A Sword Will Pierce Your Soul

A JOURNEY OF HEALING AND RESTORATION

BY CAROLINE JULIHN

A Sword Will Pierce Your Soul

Copyright © 2011 Caroline Julihn

ISBN: 978-1460948484

First Edition

Cover Design and Layout by Corey Julihn, CE Studios Inc.

Well Brad, it's no longer a pamphlet! Thank you for believing in me. Thank you for your generous and steadfast love! Thank you for being an example of grace and mercy throughout very dark and difficult days.

Derian, Allison, Shannon, Corey and Erin, thank you for your fierce loyalty to me. Thank you for being a sounding board. Thank you for your perspective and for the wisdom I have gained through your insight.

Carla and Deborah, thank you listening. Thank you for your prayers. Thank you for holding me accountable. And above all, thank you for your friendship.

In memory of my Mom

Contents

Preface

It is certainly not a grand revelation to say many pastors have left their churches under controversial and even devastating circumstances. We personally know a number of pastors and their families who have suffered great wounding as they were forced from their churches. We have heard their horror stories. They have often stood before their congregations reading their *resignation* letters when in reality they had been asked to resign. And if we were truly honest, we should say they were fired. It seems at times leadership boards hide behind these resignation letters, feigning innocence, when in fact they have not only instigated them, but insisted upon them. I have heard of boards who have threatened their pastors with no severance package unless they resign and then mandate what can or cannot be said in their resignation letters. After leaving their churches, some pastors have transitioned quickly to new ministries. Others have taken a break for awhile, returning to the pastorate at a later time. Unfortunately, we also know those who have never fully recovered and have not returned to ministry. Quite naively, I felt immune to be one of those horror stories or suffer the heartache we watched others go through. But after many years serving a church, we too experienced great wounding through our exit.

It is now several years since we left the church we spent almost seventeen years serving. To say that the final six months of our tenure were difficult would be an understatement. For me personally, this event was traumatic and I have spent years working through the aftermath of those final few months. Even now I am aware that I am still in need of a measure of healing; the journey is not yet finished. To this day, I find it difficult to understand the actions taken by some in their effort to remove my husband not only from pastoring our former church, but from ministry altogether.

Justifiably, there may be times for a church to bring a pastoral assignment to an end. Perhaps there are unhealthy or even sinful issues in the life of a pastor; perhaps it may simply be time for someone new. Sometimes to allow a pastor to say he is *resigning* is in fact, showing mercy. Whatever the reason for bringing their tenure to an end, exit strategies must be carefully considered and even more carefully implemented. A hasty or poor exit strategy is likely to wound both the pastor and the congregation. The unfortunate reality is that even the most carefully implemented plan is not a guarantee that people will not be wounded. In fact, I believe wounding at some level will occur regardless of the most carefully laid plans simply because we are human and easily hurt.

Unfortunately, when a church experiences a difficult or controversial pastoral exit it is not just the pastor and his family who will be injured. Without exception, the entire church family will face consequences. Often division will occur. When a church finally reaches this point, some will choose to leave the church. They will find new places to worship. Others will remain. They will determinedly and faithfully carry on. But certain individuals will be intensely affected by what transpired. They will struggle not only with their church experience, but their personal faith will suffer as well. Confused and angered by what they have witnessed, there is a very real danger that they will never step foot in a church again. In my mind, this is grievous!

I have been asked, why write a book dealing with such a sensitive subject matter. Why air the church's dirty laundry? Will it not just bring greater harm to the church family? Is this book in fact a vindictive act of revenge? While these are certainly legitimate concerns, it is my desire that the Lord is honored by this book in spite of the difficult subject matter. This book is not a way to exact my revenge on those who brought harm, although admittedly, my human heart would most easily and eagerly stoop to such tactics. But I am keenly aware that God loves his church. He does not attack or bring harm to his people. He does not gossip, lie or bring false accusation. He does not shame or humiliate. He always defends the truth and he asks the same of his children. Therefore, this is not a *tell all* book. Although some of the story needs to be told, the precise details of what transpired during our final months will remain largely unwritten. They are, however, forever etched in my memory. And so as I write, I find myself striving hard to maintain the balance between speaking truthfully about my experience without revealing too much. I neither want to bring accusation nor harm to a wonderful church family we spent many years serving; sixteen and a half of those years were a joy. It was an honor to serve this congregation. Even during the final grueling six months we were supported by many. I will always be grateful for those who stood with us, who fought to keep troubling behavior in check, and quietly and prayerfully watched our backs.

So why write? One evening, as I began reading the book of Luke, the phrase 'a sword will pierce your very soul' leapt off the page and into the very depths of my soul. I wept in sorrow as I recognized and identified with that pain. That night my journal holds only this question: A sword will pierce your very soul… book title? I began to reflect on this phrase. Soon it became my constant companion. Although I had never considered writing, the Lord seemed to impress this project on me. And so I began to pray, and then I began to write. This book is my story; it is written from my perspective. It is not my husband's story nor is it my family's. It is also not the story of our former church, although at times the lines are blurred simply because together, we endured a very difficult event. The purpose of this book is to speak openly and frankly about the trauma I experienced through the process of exiting our church. It is also to acknowledge my struggle with the consequences which resulted and to share my journey of healing.

Being *pierced in my soul* affected every part of my life. This book examines the physical, emotional, mental and spiritual consequences I have had to face. I've had to come to terms with serious accusations made against me. I've had to heal from the symptoms of Post Traumatic Stress Disorder. I've had to learn to trust the church again. But I have also had to acknowledge my own sin and need for cleansing. The sword that pierced my soul not only held the power to wound, but it uncovered sin which lay deep within me. I've had to face my own anger, unforgiveness and bitterness. I've had to, not only let go of grudges held, but the desire for revenge as well. I've had to slog my way to forgiveness and then struggle to come to grips with what reconciliation might look like. But most importantly, this book is a testimony to the healing I have received and the hope, that even as I write, the Lord will finish his work of restoration in me.

I have also written this book because my family is not alone. We are not the first nor will we be the last pastor's family who has experienced a devastating church exit. Many pastors and their families have faced brutal exits and many have been devastated by their experience. Families have been shattered and careers ruined. And many pastors feel that they cannot talk about the damage done not only to their ministry, but their personal lives as well. Who can you confide in? How can you heal if you cannot talk about or work through your experience? It is my hope, that as I honestly share my experience, others who have been traumatized by their church experience may find a measure of healing.

Throughout this journey I have had tremendous support from my family, both immediate and extended. I have rested in the mercy and compassion of truly great friends. I can't thank them enough for their love and grace. I have also greatly benefited from professional counseling. It was very necessary. Without it, I would not be as far down the road to recovery as I am. But ultimately, this book is my journey of prayer. It has been largely through prayer that the Lord has brought his healing to me. It is through prayer God has given me insight into the damage done to my heart, mind and soul. And through prayer, he has brought me, and continues to bring me, to places of acceptance and peace.

I believe the Lord has deeply loved and honored me as he has taken me on this journey of healing. It is my desire that he in turn would be honored as I seek to testify to his mercy and grace. Although no one would willingly choose to be pierced in their soul or incur the many consequences brought on by this wounding, I can genuinely say that I am grateful for what I've gone through. I am not the same person I once was. Granted this is both good and bad. It saddens me to have lost a measure of trust in people, and the church no longer feels as safe as it once did. At the same time I have grown to know the heart of my Savior at a deeper level. I have been made more like him. I have been the recipient of his mercy, compassion and his healing. I have gained wisdom and insight. And for these reasons I can say that being pierced in my soul was in truth a gift from God. Yes, it came disguised in a most cruel and ugly form. And yes, it caused undeniable and permanent damage but in the Saviors hand, what men, women and demons used to bring harm, God used to bring healing, transformation and his goodness! And he is glorified and my soul… well, my soul will sing once again!

*There is no demand made upon
my life that is not a demand
made upon the life of Christ
within me.*

*There is nothing, no circumstances,
no trouble, no testing that can
touch me until first of all,
it has gone past God and past Christ,
right through to me.*

*If it has come that far, it has come
with great purpose.*

(author unknown)

Chapter 1

Pierced In Your Soul

"This child (Jesus) will be rejected by many, and it will be their undoing. But he will be the greatest joy to many others. Thus, the deepest thoughts of many hearts will be revealed and a sword will pierce your very soul!" (Luke 2:35).

These are the prophetic words spoken by Simeon over Mary as she and Joseph brought Jesus into the temple to present the purification offering and to dedicate him to God. As I read the last phrase of that verse again, "and a sword will pierce your very soul", my heart cried out: I know what that piercing feels like! I have felt the sting of that blade! I have suffered the consequences of that terrible sword! I wept in sorrow as words were finally given to the deep and lasting pain I had been feeling. Even now the tears come. It is hard to contain them. They come at the most inopportune times. The memory of that vile blade awakens the anguish in my soul yet again.

The most extreme wounding I have known came through the process of exiting the church my husband and I spent seventeen years serving. The final six months of our tenure were both shocking and devastating. During those months we came under intense scrutiny and criticism. Serious accusations were leveled against me. Our reputations were tarnished, our ministry questioned, and my husband's career was put in jeopardy. I left the church broken and deeply traumatized. It is years later and I am still recovering from the conflict of those few months. But I should not have been surprised by this very difficult time for the Lord had warned us on a number of occasions, just a few months earlier, of a time of suffering that was approaching. During our times of prayer, the Lord cautioned us that he was stirring up a hornets' nest and that it would get ugly for a time. He encouraged us that though criticism would come, he had equipped and strengthened us to receive it and not be bowed low beneath its weight. We were even warned that criticism would be leveled against me and that criticism would ultimately have a bearing on my husband. We were told this would be a time of injustice and we were not to be surprised by it. We were to fix our eyes on Jesus for he was able to carry us through this time. He knew all about suffering and was able to teach us much for he had endured suffering and great injustice as well. He encouraged us not to be afraid for he had been preparing us for this time. He would endure with us, stand with us and would be a shield about us.

Although we were forewarned of this impending time of suffering and injustice, I did not fully grasp the significance of those warnings. It is only now as I look back at my journal entries that I recognize the full implication and meaning of those warnings. I am amazed at how precise and accurate they were. I wish that I could say, since we had ample warning of what was about to take place, that I walked through this dark time in confidence and with my head held high, but the truth is I did not. Not only was I short sighted as to the significance of these warnings, but I failed to keep them in mind. I was so overwhelmed by the brutal exit strategy and evaluation process that for a time, I was bowed low beneath the weight of criticism and the harmful actions of certain individuals. In truth, I was crushed and devastated!

And so that evening as I began to read Luke this little phrase, a sword will pierce your very soul, leapt off the page at me. Although my heart cried out in recognition of being pierced in my soul, I cannot make a case that I indeed was. I cannot even accurately define or characterize what being pierced in your soul is. Is it even definable? The soul is one of those deep God mysteries theologians have debated about for hundreds of years. It is my understanding the soul is the very makeup or composition of a person. It is the foundation of who we are. It is what makes you different from anyone else. The soul is how you relate to others and how you understand yourself. It is distinct and separate from our physical body, yet very much part of life, feeling and thought. The soul comprises all of who you are and it is clear from scripture that our souls can be pierced and therefore, wounded.

Although I cannot clearly define what being pierced in your soul is, I am confident that it is not simply a glancing blow. It is not a flesh wound. It is not just the quick sharp pinch of an ear or body piercing. Although it may be a quick thrust, you are not merely left with red, hot ears for a few minutes. You are left in excruciating pain that will not go away. There is a shocking quality to this sword. It overpowers and it devastates. It invades and pervades every part of your life and your being. Its blade will penetrate through you; through all your defenses, and lodge itself in the deepest, most private, holy and sacred parts of your being. This sword touches and wounds everything that comprises who you are. And when this sword has finished its work, you will not be the same person you once were. Not ever!

When someone experiences a tragic or catastrophic event we instinctively understand their wounds may have life altering and devastating consequences. To put it another way, they will have received soul piercing injuries. A few examples of such catastrophic events would include the loss of a child, a horrific accident, war or rape. We recognize the magnitude of these events will affect everything that comprises that person. We instinctively understand those who suffer such injury may never be the same. We know they may never fully recover from such terrible wounding. But strangely enough there are some individuals who are not profoundly injured nor are they pierced in their soul, despite experiencing devastating and tragic events. It is as though this sword is somehow powerless to do the damage it was meant to do. Take, for example, Horatio G. Spafford who penned the famous hymn, 'It Is Well With My Soul,' just weeks after all four of his daughters died when the ship they were on collided with another. Through his grief and devastating loss he was able say, "it is well with my soul", and carry on with life and ministry. But there are many who, having experienced this level of tragedy, could not have recovered enough to carry on with their lives, jobs and ministries.

Just as some souls are not pierced through catastrophic events, others will be pierced by what we might consider a minor event. Some may in fact find a relatively minor event to be traumatic and devastating. Although the actual event or incident may be trivial, it essentially becomes catastrophic simply because of the enormous affect it has on an individual. Whether the event is disastrous or insignificant, it is impossible to predict the impact it will have on an individual. Unfortunately, because an event is not seen as catastrophic, some may question the intensity of the pain felt by an individual. They may wonder why they are playing a victim's role and why they "can't just get over it." After all, what happened wasn't so terrible. But we cannot simply brush aside someone's pain. We dare not think we can be the judge of how deeply an individual should have been impacted. No two people will respond to being wounded in the same way. The same sword may strike, leaving one person seemingly unscathed by it, while another will be completely struck down.

Our exit from the church was not a tragic or catastrophic event. My husband was relatively unscathed, though not untouched by our exit. I, on the other hand, find myself still lying in the dust looking for the box of Kleenex. My husband is not living in denial of what happened. He too has had to face the same consequences as I have. He does not have impregnable skin. He is not hard hearted. No, the sword was thrust just as deeply, but somehow for him the injury was not as great. At times I've thought to myself, Lord, what is wrong with that man? Why was he not more deeply wounded? Is he oblivious to how much damage was done? I've actually been frustrated with him. At the same time I am sure my husband has been concerned about the length of time my healing has taken. And I am also sure he has wondered how we could afford all the Kleenex I was going through. We have finally just accepted the fact that during this event my husband's soul remained intact; whole and well. My soul, on the other hand, was pierced and severely damaged. One event; two completely different responses to it!

Every member of our family was wounded during our church exit. Some in our family walked away with minor wounds while others were devastated. Although each of us experienced varying degrees of wounding, we all recognize that our church exit played a pivotal role in shaping our family today. This event has become an epoch; a significant moment in time by which we now distinguish all other events. We remember people, travel, weddings etc by whether the event happened while we were at the church or after we left. It is as though this event denotes the BC and AD of our calendar.

We also discovered that expectations for healing and moving forward were directly related to our level of pain. My husband, because he was not deeply injured, was ready to jump right back into ministry and assumed I would also be ready. But as the weeks and months went by we recognized I was anything but ready. I was deeply traumatized and therefore we simply had to take a step back. Church was no longer a safe place for me. I could probably count on one hand, the number of times I attended a service the first year after our departure. Church had become a place where I was constantly looking over my shoulder; feeling anxious, panicked and overwhelmed. Songs would bring a flood of tears. I didn't want to talk to anyone. I just wanted to run out and never look back.

Although we kept pursuing permanent ministry, I knew we could not move forward until I could heal enough to find a measure of safety within the church. Thankfully the Lord provided an interim position for my husband. We found ourselves at a small church which had also been terribly wounded. Since this was an interim position we did not need to candidate. I consider that a gift. Quite honestly I could not have survived the candidating process of another church. I could not have faced the legitimate scrutiny a potential pastor is put through. Although there were many Sundays I struggled to go, the people of this church loved us and probably unbeknownst to many, were used of God to bring a measure of healing to me. They, very slowly, became safe! They had few expectations. They were just grateful to have a pastor. They thought very highly of my husband and took every opportunity to acknowledge him. They were generous with their encouragement, generous with our salary and generous in bestowing gifts on us, both monetary and otherwise. They were the epitome of Hebrews 10: 24 where it says "Think of ways to encourage one another to outbursts of love and good deeds." And what is more, they wanted us to stay on permanently. So much so, they even offered us a signing bonus! WOW! Have you ever heard of a pastor being offered a signing bonus? But my husband and I knew God's call to this church was and always had been a temporary assignment. And so after two and half years, it was time to move on. It was very hard for me to leave this church. I had found a place of safety among them and they also gained a measure of healing during our time there. To me this was victory! And when we left, true to the nature of this church, we were lovingly roasted, given gifts and given a most generous bonus to boot. It was given in love for us and at great sacrifice to them. I am still wowed and incredibly grateful to the people in this congregation. Their kindness and generous encouragement was something I desperately needed after feeling so beaten down, by some, in our former church.

It is without question that being pierced in your soul causes profound wounding with deep and lasting results. As my own journey of healing has grown from months into years I have realized that recovering from wounds is only one part of being pierced in my soul. The sword that is capable of piercing souls aspires to bring greater harm than wounding alone. It searches for ways to harden your heart against both God and those who wielded the sword. It wants to embitter you against God for allowing so much pain. And it wants to poison you against those who wielded the sword for causing so much pain. But the truth is God allows terrible things to happen. He allows swift and terrible swords to strike us. He is not taken by surprise by the tremendous damage this sword is capable of inflicting. He is well aware, everything that comprises who we are will be touched. He knows that it is in those places of agonizing pain and suffering that our true character will be revealed. Pain will not allow pretense. Who we really are will be exposed and we will be forced to confront that which lies deep within. When my soul was pierced it uncovered and unleashed hatred, rage, unforgiveness and a desire for revenge. I was not only surprised at what lurked deep within, but what I was capable of doing to others. And I was grieved and broken.

Not only is it the goal of this sword to embitter you against God and those who inflicted the wounds, but it wants to re-shape you into its image. It wants to keep you living in woundedness so that ultimately you begin to pierce the souls of others; that in your pain, you bring pain to others. If your soul cannot heal, all your relationships will, to some degree, be affected. If your soul cannot heal, the repercussions of unresolved hurt will, in some way, touch everything you do for the rest of your life. It is as though a dark shadow is cast over you. This shadow may not be obvious or clearly defined, but it is nonetheless always there. It may take subtle forms of depression, anxiety, fear, resentment, bitterness or anger. The connection between these feelings and the wounds received in the past may never be made. That being the case, you will simply continue to live in woundedness; your soul robbed of joy and life itself.

We should neither be surprised nor angry that God allows devastating wounds to touch our lives. We should not be surprised that God uses pain and suffering to reveal our true character. It is our character that is of the utmost importance to God. Our character is meant to reflect him in all things and at all times. Although terrible pain and suffering may be imposed upon us, ultimately we are wounded in order to make us more like our Savior.

Although God allows swift and terrible swords to strike us he does not abandon us to this wounding. It is not his desire for us to remain in a place of devastation. He does not want us to live with a dark shadow cast over our lives because we are unable to heal from the trauma we've experienced. God desires to heal the brokenhearted, to lift up the humble and to set prisoners free. It is his longing to restore our soul. But strangely enough, he will permit you the choice of how far you allow him to take you on the journey of healing. He always waits for our co-operation, as though the journey is a partnership. The choice is ours whether we will submit to this time of testing and suffering. It is our choice whether we will allow our character to be developed. The choice is ours whether we will allow God to cleanse us of hidden and deeply buried sin. The choice is ours whether we will allow him to heal us and restore our soul.

I have found God to be a faithful and gentle healer, but I have also been surprised to discover that healing is far more difficult than I could have ever imagined. Healing will not happen overnight. God allows us to live in deep pain for a very long time. He does not do quick fixes. He is gentle, but he is thorough. And we must both understand and accept that it takes a great deal of time and effort for our soul to heal when it has been profoundly wounded. The journey of healing will require courage, persistence, faith and much prayer. My own recovery has been surprisingly slow. It has taken years of hard work. But I have learned not to feel guilty about the length of time it has taken to heal. I have learned to not feel pushed by the spoken or unspoken expectations, mine or someone else's, for healing. I have learned not to have expectations of what the healing process should look like, how long it should take, or even what the final outcome will look like. I have recognized that having a time line for healing is unrealistic. And unrealistic expectations only add to the feelings of guilt. In the end, it only brings more harm. The journey will be sabotaged and healing will take longer.

It is through the process of healing that I've learned a great deal not only about myself but others as well. I have grown in my knowledge and love for Jesus. I have been made more like him as I've confronted hidden and deeply buried sin. My character has begun to reflect him more. I have watched as he has brought good out of the destructive actions taken by some in our former church. I have seen God bring good out of evil. Although my journey of healing is not yet over, I have not remained bowed low beneath the weight of accusation and criticism. And as my soul continues to be restored I have come to greater places of acceptance and peace. My soul has found rest and healing.

Chapter 2

UNFAITHFUL WOUNDS

"Faithful are the wounds of a friend." (Proverbs 27:6 NASB)

You can be sure that when there is division within a church, through the exchange of heated words and hasty actions taken, wounds were inflicted. We, the Church, are quite adept at dishonoring and wounding one another through unguarded and angry words and accusations. We gossip, we criticize, we blame, we exaggerate and we even lie about one another. We make our assumptions and pronounce our judgments often based on hearsay and gossip. Through pride and selfish ambition we manipulate visions and agendas into place mowing down anyone who stands in our way. I believe these actions to be characteristic of unfaithful wounds and they are often at the core of division within a church.

It seems division will often revolve around a pastor in some way or another. Sometimes, as new visions or new ministries are considered the question may arise whether the current pastor is the right person to lead the church forward in implementing them. This is a valid question to ask. It should not surprise us if we have different opinions on the matter. It should also not surprise us that heated words may be exchanged through the evaluation process. This can be appropriate and even fitting. But if the tension and conflict escalates or if agendas and visions are hastily pushed through, a church will find itself standing at the precipice of division. At this point it is likely that pastors will be asked to resign. The church will finally be pushed to its breaking point and people will begin leaving.

There is no doubt that evaluating a pastor will have a polarizing effect on a church. It is natural for the congregation to align themselves with either the pastor or those seeking his removal. Although some may try to remain neutral, the truth is, it is almost impossible to remain impartial. In reality, everyone will be dragged into the conflict in some way even if it is only to ask themselves, do I stay? Do I quietly slip out the door? Do I leave until this mess is over and re-evaluate when the new pastor arrives? Certainly in the end, all will be forced to make a choice.

As we found ourselves lined up in the cross hairs of those initiating our removal, we faced a very grueling and confusing time in our lives. I felt as though we were put in a vulnerable and indefensible position. Once loved and respected we now encountered a hostile, even caustic environment. Impatient to implement a new vision, those planning our departure seemed to give little or no thought to a good exit strategy. This impatience led to impulsive decision making and edicts which were decreed with little concern for the church or for us. Every flaw seemed to be thoroughly scrutinized and our imperfections were exaggerated as concerns were raised with the congregation. Sermons once appreciated were now viewed with suspicion and criticism. At times I felt those seeking our removal resorted to coercion or manipulation to achieve their desired goal. I felt verbally beaten down as accusations were leveled. My husband's ministry and career was threatened. And in the end we were given a quick farewell lunch with a few speeches and a token gift. It became most painful as those we had considered friends treated us with wariness and disdain. Somehow we had become their adversary; someone to get rid of. It felt as though we were escorted, or rather pushed, to the nearest exit by them with the doors of the church slamming shut so fast behind us, they almost clipped our heels.

As difficult as this process was on us, I want to acknowledge, it was also a very painful and confusing time for our former church family. The evaluation process weighed heavily on them as they grappled with the issues before them. I believe that most in the church never wanted the conflict or upheaval. It was neither their desire nor their intent to divide the church. And I believe most worked hard to both protect and honor the church as well as our family during this time.

I have realized that a lingering consequence of division is *confusion*. Although this may seem like a deviation from the topic of unfaithful wounds, I felt it was important to acknowledge this long term effect on the church. Time and again I have had individuals confess how confused they felt as their churches faced division. They have stated that although it had been years since the conflict took place, they still did not have a clear picture as to what really happened and they still felt confused by the whole ordeal. I believe one reason for the confusion may be that congregations are rarely given the full details as to what is being discussed behind closed doors. Sometimes little or no information is shared. I believe the underlying reason for this is to protect both the pastor and the church body. It is seen as protecting the rights and reputation of an individual, but it is also meant to curb rumors and gossip within the church. While it is certainly unnecessary to make every detail public, there is also the complex issue of privacy and confidentiality laws which must be considered and adhered to. At heart, being prudent about the information shared with the congregation is a good principle. It may indeed graciously protect an individual's reputation, but I must admit I am reticent to fully embrace secrecy where sin is concerned. I am uncertain that sin should be protected. I am also uncertain whether rumors and gossip are curbed by secrecy. I wonder if in fact this principle not only allows a church leader to continue in their sin, but actually precipitates or encourages gossip and unnecessarily creates confusion within the church. When a congregation does not have adequate information or a clear understanding of the issues it is natural for them to begin to talk to one another and it is only a matter of time before the rumors will start. One person will have heard a certain report while another will have heard something completely different. Any conclusions drawn will largely depend on the perspective or opinion of the person an individual has talked to. Unfortunately, that person's perspective may be biased and even incorrect. It is difficult for the church to find truth in secrecy, gossip and confusion.

There is no doubt that there is a fine line between respecting the legal confidentiality rights of an individual and the right for the congregation to be given both correct and good information. Without question those in leadership face a daunting task as they grapple with the complexity of this issue. Nevertheless, I believe that it is vital for leaders to make every effort to be as forthright as possible with their congregation so that they are not left shrouded in rumor, innuendo and confusion; angry with one another and not really knowing the truth as to why certain decisions were made or why their pastor left.

That issue aside, I am certain we as believers understand that we dishonor both God and the church through division. We wound one another deeply and yet rarely ask ourselves why. What motivates us to bring harm to another? What is it that precipitates a friend, co-worker or even a co-pastor to behave in a manner which destroys that friendship or working relationship? What finally pushes someone to leave a church they have been part of for many years?

As I have reflected on these questions, I have come to the conclusion that during times of conflict and controversy there are some individuals who recklessly wound others simply because they get caught up in the heat of the moment. Some wound because they have an axe to grind and a public attack may be a way to air their grievances. Still others have an agenda to push through and they allow no one to stand in their way. I believe some injure others unintentionally; some injure foolishly while others injure without mercy.

We inflict wounds on one another and feel quite justified in doing so. Our sword of choice may be gossip, criticism, condemnation, slander, shame, manipulation or deception. But sadly, in our pride, we neither recognize nor acknowledge the harm brought to an individual or to the church body as a whole. Although we have many swords to choose from I have elected to take a closer look at only a few.

THE SWORD OF AMBITION:

I believe often at the core of unfaithful wounds lies ambition. Ambitious people may desire to move the church forward with new ideas, a new vision and in a new direction. Ambition certainly moves people and organizations forward. It can be appropriate and even necessary. But when ambition is rooted in pride, envy or the desire for power, unfaithful wounds will be inflicted every time. In many churches it is another leader or co-pastor who takes up the sword of ambition. Perhaps, they reason, the time has come for them to lead the church; it is time for a new direction. It is time for a new vision to be implemented. And so the seeds of discontentment spring to life. As the discontentment grows the grumbling begins. Grumbling turns to gossip and gossip gives way to undermining the ministry of the one seen to be in the way. The person who undermines another does so in secret. It is manipulative and deceptive work. Phone calls may be instigated or secret meetings held. There are quiet whispers and huddles in the hallway as plans are hatched. Whether done consciously or not, the goal of someone who undermines another is to win the hearts of others and gain a following. Such a person may genuinely believe they should be the one to move the church forward. They may also believe they are implementing God's vision for the church. But there is just no escaping the whiff of deceit and hint of dishonesty in such behind the scenes maneuvering. We cannot for one moment believe that gossiping, scheming or undermining the ministry of another achieves the purposes of God. I would also add that if a vision has to be manipulated and maneuvered into place that it is most likely not God's vision for the church.

The person wielding a sword of ambition will always wound unfaithfully and bring harm to the church. They are in fact, attempting to seize that which has neither been given nor entrusted to them. This sword is bathed in pride and selfish ambition. I would dare call it a sword of mutiny. And it is the rally cry for division.

The Sword of Malice:

Unfortunately there are individuals, who use the sword of malice to strike others. In their haste to implement their vision for the church few are left standing. They attack with purposeful blows as if to inflict the most severe wounds possible against those opposing their agenda. They pierce with such viciousness that, at times, it is difficult to comprehend they are in fact believers. Their actions are aggressive and demeaning. They bully and threaten. They accuse and it doesn't really matter whether the accusations are true or not. They strike with little thought. They care little whether someone is destroyed by their actions. It does not matter how many are wounded; how many are caught in the crossfire. It is of no concern if characters are assassinated, reputations are tarnished and the church is divided. The end seems to justify the means. They run roughshod over others because their agenda takes precedence over the welfare of the church family. They take no note of those who will never enter a church again because they have witnessed ungodly behavior and the church has become everything they feared. They show no concern that a good pastor may never take another church again because they or their families have been fatally wounded. They do not count the cost of the years it will take a church to recover.

The sword of malice is cruel and vindictive. It shows no mercy. It seeks not only to wound, but to bring ruin to the one it strikes. It always wounds unfaithfully. Those wielding this sword seem unaware their actions will cause a ripple effect even they cannot control. And although they may think it a feather in their cap when they are successful in their bid to remove their pastor, they would be wise to consider that the feather in their cap may just become a millstone around their neck. They cannot anticipate the damage they may bring not only upon the church, but themselves as well. I have personally witnessed this sword strike only once and I am therefore hopeful that it has rarely been used in the church.

THE SWORD OF BETRAYAL:

Although the sword of malice strikes without mercy and seeks to bring ruin to another, for me personally, the most painful and damaging wounds were delivered by the sword of betrayal. Betrayal is a most painful and cruel injury. The individual who strikes another in betrayal is in fact making the choice to terminate that relationship. The wounds inflicted are not meant to be superficial. They are intended to be fatal. I believe the individual who strikes in betrayal is false and deceptive. They hatch their plans in secret and execute them behind the backs of their intended victims. Those wielding this sword deliver their blow in surprise. Their blade is thrust in rejection. And their victim is always blindsided. Those pierced by this sword are left dazed and confused. They are shamed and humiliated. Trust is shattered. Sadly, it will most often be your closest friends who will strike in betrayal. They will deliver the most lethal blows. They are, after all, the ones standing next to you. They have the clearest shot. Their blade will penetrate the deepest simply because of the love and trust once shared through friendship. I have learned that the greater the trust given to someone, the greater the effect their betrayal will have on you.

The sword of betrayal is a sword of death. It strikes with deadly accuracy. Its wounds are the most unfaithful of all. I believe it is most difficult not only to overcome the pain and agony of being betrayed, but also to forgive those who struck in betrayal.

Faithful Wounds:

Not all wounds inflicted should be considered wrong or unfaithfully given. Proverbs 27:6 says, "Faithful are the wounds of a friend" (NASB). Psalm 141:5 says, "Let the godly strike me! It will be a kindness! If they reprove me, it is soothing medicine. Don't let me refuse it." These verses tell us that we can wound or rebuke one another and it is appropriate, right and even good. Faithful wounds are inflicted for the purpose of correction, teaching, refining and character building. These wounds are necessary to hold one another accountable to the body of Christ and enable us to grow in truth and in godliness. They are meant to deepen our friendships, not destroy them. Faithful wounds are given in humility, from those who genuinely love us and desire the very best for us. Those who wound faithfully do so carefully and with godly accuracy. Their sword is not used impulsively. They do not strike out of envy, ambition, selfishness, pride, revenge or in betrayal. They do not wound with information gathered from sweet morsels of gossip or bits of hearsay.

There is no doubt that it is sometimes difficult to distinguish whether we have been faithfully or unfaithfully wounded. Wounds are painful, whether given faithfully or not. When we are in pain, we often get defensive and we become angry with the one who has wounded us. Foolishly, we may choose to ignore or discount valid criticism and in pride rebuff it. But we would be wise to take some time to consider the correction or rebuke given. Even unfaithful wounds can bear a seed of truth and we can therefore learn from it. Proverbs 25:12 says, "Valid criticism is as treasured by the one who heeds it as jewelry made from finest gold" (NLT). Faithful wounds are treasure and we are wise to receive it as such. It is wisdom not only to value the correction, but the friend who has the courage to inflict such wounds. Their wounding comes in the form of true friendship. It is a rare and wonderful gift to have a friend who will, when necessary, unsheathe their sword of correction or rebuke and wound us because they love us and desire the very best for us.

When we face times of conflict and controversy—when we are in the midst of division and we find ourselves taking up arms—we would be wise to stop and look at the sword we are unsheathing. We would be wise to consider whether *faithful* is etched into our blade or *unfaithful* is chiseled out in its place. When we gossip, undermine or sabotage the ministry of others, we are holding an unfaithful sword. When we have to resort to hatching our plans in secret, we are holding an unfaithful sword. When we manipulate or deceive others we are wielding an unfaithful sword. When we slander or falsely accuse others; when our objective is to criticize and find fault with others we are holding an unfaithful sword. When we threaten and bully, we are clutching an unfaithful sword. When we strike in betrayal *unfaithful* is carved into our blade. These swords are not wielded in love. They are not unsheathed for noble or godly purposes. They are not just. They do not come to teach or correct. Rather these swords come to injure and to destroy. These are the swords of division. At times the cruel and deceptive quality to these swords seems to be strengthened by the pit of hell itself, for Satan delights when such unfaithful wounding takes place. We should not be surprised that he has taken an active role in dividing the church. It may take years for a pastor and his family to recover. It may also take years for a church to recover and move forward with any effectiveness. Unfortunately, some may never fully recover. For some, the wounds are fatal!

I believe it is noteworthy to consider that during times of division all will be affected and wounded. No one will escape, including those instigating or at the root of the division. It is also noteworthy to consider that whether we are the one wielding a sword or the one who has been pierced by a sword, our flaws will be exposed; our character will be revealed. Conflict and controversy within a church will test all our hearts and will reveal that which lies deep within us. We are indeed fortunate if we are never tested in this way and if we never have to confront what we are capable of doing.

Chapter 3

CHILDREN OF SAMSON AND DELILAH

I know a man who had spent time as a pastor in various churches and was part of the leadership team in others. He considered himself to be both a visionary thinker and leader, but at times I found his behavior baffling and troubling. There were periods in his life where he was a genuinely caring and spiritual man. His abilities and passion allowed him to serve in areas few of us would or could engage in. But oddly enough there were also times that I would question whether he was even a believer. He could show great mercy, but then just as quickly he would become mean and vindictive. He could become harsh and cruel in his remarks, leaving people hurt and offended. Sometimes he would manipulate the truth, resorting to deceptive tactics to achieve his goals. He also had a habit of sullying the reputations of leaders he served with, never failing to point out their shortcomings. He was quick to find something flawed with their style of leadership. He was also a part of, if not initiating, division within some churches. Unfortunately he didn't seem to see anything wrong with this and it appeared to me that he actually enjoyed the chaos he created. I saw his life as a paradox, one full of contradiction and incongruity.

I was so troubled by this individual's behavior that I wondered if he was a sheep, a wolf in sheep's clothing or a sheep with really, really sharp teeth. I spent many months in prayer bringing him before the Lord. I was troubled by the fact that overall his life seemed to lack consistency and integrity. His spiritual life was predictably inconsistent and yet he not only remained, but tightly held on to leadership roles within the church. I was frustrated that such a volatile and harmful person was successful in both leading and dividing the church. In my mind this man was neither a visionary thinker nor a visionary leader. For many months I asked the Lord: Is he blind to the terrible wounds he inflicts? Is he not conflicted by the inconsistency of his life? Lord, does he truly believe that he is implementing your will and vision through deception? And what about his lack of integrity? What about the compromises in his life? What about the times he bullies others? Does he not feel any sorrow or remorse for the division he is creating? Is he even a believer? I asked these questions over and over again as I struggled to gain some understanding. The answers simply eluded me. I was stymied. Finally, one evening as I once again found myself praying for this man and brought these questions before the Lord, I received a strange and unexpected response. *He is a son of Samson and Delilah!* What? What son? There is no mention of Samson and Delilah having a son! Did I really hear that? I was ready to dismiss this thought as just my imagination, but as I reflected on Samson's life, I began to see the connection. As strange as it initially seemed, I soon realized why this was indeed the answer to the questions I had been asking the Lord.

We find the story of Samson recorded in the book of Judges. We learn that an angel of the Lord was sent to a barren woman to bring her the wonderful news that she would have a son. She was told this son was to be set apart for God as a Nazirite. As a Nazirite, Samson had to follow strict rules such as abstaining from alcohol, he was never to touch a dead body and he could never cut his hair. While most Nazirite vows were taken for a limited period, there are two cases recorded in scripture of lifelong Nazirites; one being Samson the other, Samuel. Not only was Samson a Nazirite, he was appointed by God to be a judge for the nation Israel. Beyond judicial responsibilities, judges were both military and political leaders. They not only presided over the courts and made important rulings for the nation, they were also warriors used by God to mete out his judgment against the foreign invaders and oppressors of Israel. God had given Samson unusually great strength as a way to mete out his judgment against the Philistines. Samson was in fact, so successful in slaying Philistines, that he soon became their great enemy. He even made it on to their number one most wanted list. God had placed a high call on Samson's life. He had been given both authority and ability to lead and serve the nation Israel. In Hebrews 11:32 Samson is cited, along with those of great faith, who advanced the kingdom of God. He is among the "great cloud of witnesses" whose lives of faith encourage us to press on in our own walk of faith.

I remember being taught the story of Samson and Delilah in Sunday School. It is one of the more memorable stories we learned. As children, we were taught to revere Samson as one empowered with great strength to do mighty works for God. Samson was depicted much like a super hero who took on lions with his bare hands and conquered his evil enemies. In a lapse of judgment he was tricked by the charms of a wicked woman and taken captive. Evil triumphed for a time, but in the end, Samson died a heroic death while killing many evil Philistines. As a child I was quite impressed with Samson and felt quite angry that he was tricked by such an evil woman. But I must confess, as an adult, I now see Samson in quite a different light. He no longer holds that faultless super hero status as seen through the eyes of a child. I now see him as someone with a cavalier attitude toward God's gifting and call on his life. Although scripture tells us that Samson was indeed chosen of God, and that the Spirit of God took hold of him in order for God's purposes for Israel to be fulfilled, I do not believe he fully lived in submission to God. Sadly that lack of submission led him to behave in compromising ways. He was full of pride, bad tempered, impulsive, selfish, and immoral. He fraternized with the enemy, slept with a prostitute, deceived others and was himself easily deceived. In my opinion he did not carry out judgment on the Philistines out of concern for the nation Israel, rather he pursued his own agenda and built his own empire. He did not lead or serve the nation of Israel through righteous or just acts of judgment. His leadership was birthed in pride, personal gain and revenge. Many scholars do not believe he remained faithful to the Nazirite vow he was bound to from conception. I find myself amazed that God continued to use Samson in spite of his ongoing compromising behavior. I find it even more remarkable that he is given a place of honor among the great cloud of witnesses in Hebrews.

Perhaps you are surprised by my lack of admiration for Samson. Perhaps you don't remember him in this way and still hold him in high esteem. If that is the case, permit me to retell at least part of the story of Samson and Delilah.

One fine day, while Samson was wandering the countryside, he caught a glimpse of a Philistine woman. There was an instant attraction! He saw her, he wanted her and he insisted on marrying her. But this woman was part of the pagan nation that was oppressing Israel and so Samson's parents strenuously objected to this marriage. Samson was not about to be swayed by their disapproval, so they finally relented and made the necessary arrangements. During the pre-wedding festivities Samson made a foolish bet, and through the trickery of his fiancé, lost that bet. He was furious! But not to be out witted, he killed thirty Philistines. He stripped them of their clothes and paid the debt he owed. He was so enraged by these events that he promptly left his fiancé and returned home to mom and dad to sulk. After a short cooling off period he went back to claim his bride only to find that she had been given in marriage to his best man. He was incensed and decided to once again, take matter into his own hands. He caught three hundred foxes, tied their tails together in pairs and fastened a torch to each pair of tails. Lighting the torches, he let the blazing foxes loose in the fields of the Philistines. Their vineyards, fields of grain and olive trees were burned to the ground. The Philistines retaliated by burning Samson's ex-fiancé and her father to death. Samson then evened the score by slaughtering more Philistines.

Samson loved women. Perhaps one could even call him a womanizer. He was sexually immoral, spending the night with a prostitute. Eventually, Samson met and fell in love with Delilah. The Philistines offered Delilah a great deal of money to uncover the secret of Samson's strength. Throughout his life, Samson held tightly to the secret that his strength was tied to his hair. No hair, no strength. Delilah begged and pleaded with Samson to give up his secret, but he would not reveal it. The fact is he repeatedly lied to her, telling her he had to be tied up in certain ways for his strength to fail. Delilah believed Samson's lies and she made several attempts to betray him to the Philistines; for a price of course. Each attempt was futile. I cannot understand why Samson failed to see Delilah's treachery. The multiple attempts to capture him were made in her home. Surely his suspicions should be raised after the second attempt was made. I also find myself troubled by the fact that Samson was having sleepovers at his girlfriend's house. I am troubled by the fact that Samson did not awaken as he was being tied up or while his hair was being tugged at as it was woven into fabric. Could it be that he was in fact in a drunken stupor? Was it possible to sleep so soundly through all that jostling without being drunk? And poor Delilah! She was beginning to look foolish to her co-conspirators after all the failed attempts to capture Samson. She soon became frantic! There was a large amount of money at stake! How could she get Samson to tell her the true source of his strength? She finally resorted to using all her feminine wiles, namely nagging, to wear Samson down. At long last he could no longer stand it and finally let the cat out of the bag. So while he once again slept soundly, his head was shaved. His strength was now truly gone and he was unable to fend off the Philistines. They gouged out is eyes and imprisoned him.

After some time had passed the Philistines held a great celebration in the temple of their god Dagon. They were praising Dagon for giving them victory over their great enemy Samson. Samson, with his hair now grown back, was brought to the temple where the people began to mock him. And as he stood center stage, Samson prayed that God would remember him and strengthen him once more. He then put his hands on the center pillars of the temple and pushed against them with all his might. God heard Samson's prayer and the temple collapsed, killing Samson and thousands of

Philistines. Ah, what victory! But please take note, even in death Samson's prayer was for himself alone. He did not ask God to strengthen him again and use him to free Israel from the oppressive rule of the Philistines. No, he asked that God would strengthen him once more so that he could pay back the Philistines for the loss of his eyes. It was a selfish prayer for himself. It was a prayer for revenge. And surprisingly enough, God answered it.

As my thoughts turned back to the man I had been praying about, I no longer questioned that strange response I had heard during my time of prayer. I had to concede that this man was indeed a son of Samson and Delilah. The resemblance had become quite obvious. Both he and Samson were called and gifted to lead; Samson for a nation, this particular individual for the church. And although both certainly had some success in their ministry, their lives were nonetheless marred by careless and inconsistent behavior, selfishness, pride and compromise. At times their leadership looked more like impulsive random acts rather than visionary, insightful or Spirit-filled actions taken for those they served. They seemed more concerned with their own agenda; building their own empires rather than advancing God's Kingdom.

In the third chapter of 1 Timothy, scripture speaks to us about the qualifications for church leaders. Among other things, it tells us that an elder must be someone whose life cannot be spoken against; both in the church and outside the church. They must be someone who exhibits self-control, lives wisely, and has a good reputation. Likewise, deacons must be people who are respected and have integrity. They must not be heavy drinkers or greedy for money. These qualifications are not given with the expectation of perfection; rather they are speaking to the character qualities of godly leaders. I believe that God is especially concerned with the character of those who lead and shepherd our churches. Scripture says they are held to a higher account. It is therefore wise for churches to take the time to test their leaders according to the guidelines set out for us in scripture. Sadly, the reality is, even testing our leaders is not a guarantee of godly leadership.

I believe that as a church, we are concerned with the character of those who lead us. We desire godly men and women to teach and lead us. But I wonder if we have not confused godly leadership with *visionary* leadership. Vision casting or being visionary has become the Holy Grail in our churches today. It seems every church wants their leaders to be visionary; men and women who will effect change with the hope that the church will grow. I believe both the emphasis and expectation to have visionary leaders may in fact be detrimental. It is detrimental not because being visionary is wrong, but because we have a false belief or understanding as to what being visionary really is. We often equate successful or visionary leadership with church growth; an increase in numbers. We believe that we are being visionary when in fact all we have done is implement ideas and programs that have successfully grown other churches into mega-churches. But can we really consider ourselves visionary when in reality we have done nothing more than to buy some books and implement someone else's teaching? Are we not simply buying a franchise or using a cookie cutter to try and re-create similar results? Being a visionary leader has little to do with implementing ideas or programs which were successful in other churches. It is not about growing our churches into mega-churches. This type of vision requires little faith, little prayer and little work. It is more likely human effort and man-made vision; empire building instead of Kingdom building.

I believe the Church today is in need of visionary leaders! But just exactly what is a visionary leader? My definition of true visionary leader is that they will not only have the godly characteristics as laid out for us in scripture, but they will also be men and women of prayer. I believe that being truly visionary is all about prayer. If we seriously desire God's vision for the Church, we will recognize that it will come through men and women who have waited on the Lord in prayer. God will reveal his vision through humble servants; those who are obedient, those who have faith and most likely, those who have endured suffering. We need only look back on history at the lives of those who affected great change for both the Church and for the nations of the world. Their prayers, obedience, faith and suffering resulted in revivals and ministries which impacted the nations. They were not interested in building their own empires; rather they desired to advance God's Kingdom. George Müller, Brother Lawrence, Madame Jeanne Guyon and Rees Howells are just a few examples of those God used to accomplish great things for his Kingdom.

I believe leaders who think that they are visionary when in reality they are merely concerned with pushing through their own ideas and agenda or implementing someone else's teaching and vision are in fact harmful to the church. In their pride and haste to move the church forward they take on the characteristics of the children of Samson and Delilah. In the end they run roughshod over their congregations, leaving them confused and angry. They often fire their pastors because they no longer fit in with the new direction the church is heading. Pastors suddenly find themselves reading their resignation letters and the church family is left fractured and divided. Unfortunately, human vision and empire building only paves the way to division within the church.

Just this week we learned of two pastors whose resignations were forced. I am told it was because they no longer fit in with the new vision. In one case, a leader has been at the forefront of forcing the resignation of just about every pastor the church has ever had. Dare I say he has built his own empire and is ruling over it? Sadly, both pastors and their families were deeply wounded. To date they are no longer in ministry; one pastor has retrained while the other is in process. They both attend different churches. One weeps through the service. The other was so destroyed that his rage has turned toward his family. Perhaps one day they will find healing.

My son Derian writes a blog. In response to one of his submissions about churches in general, the spouse of a pastor who was forced to resign, had this to say:

> I just read your blog and I really connected with it. I wrote the email below to my new pastor today— I'm sharing it with you because I feel like you may understand. I don't ever want to talk about it—just be understood from afar. In psychology they say that if you keep on smiling when you are not happy eventually the emotions of happiness will follow. I guess I am hoping the same is true for faith—even when there is none, if I keep on pretending that eventually it will come. I know it's not true but I don't know what else to hope for.
>
> Dear Pastor John,
>
> I've done a lot of thinking since we talked and have come up with some answers. You asked why we kept on going to church after our previous one had wounded us and I didn't have an answer but I do now.

There are 2 reasons—because my spouse still believes in God and because if we continued attending church like nothing happened, the people at our previous church would think that they didn't hurt us and we would have the upper hand. I really have no other reasons for showing up. I quickly realized after our conversation that I had put my feelings where they were not going to disturb me and began to 'fake happy' at church again. I have realized that I really don't have a problem with Pastor Mark (new associate pastor) but rather with the fact that he is the only one that has really asked me how I am doing and I have to be fake with him to protect myself and I hate it—but I hate it because of me not because of him. I have left the church just like so many people have, I just happen to still be showing up physically. I can convince myself that I want to believe when I am at church but I leave and I'm empty and my faith is gone. I know everything in my head but all of that can be easily explained away and I just don't have it in me to care. I can talk the talk, fake it to lead a small group & to sing in the worship team but there's nothing beyond that for me and I just don't care anymore.

Laura

(names have been changed, used with permission)

We, the Church should grieve! How often has this happened because the children of Samson and Delilah are leading our churches? New ideas and visions may have been implemented; empires may have been built, and it will have come at the expense of pastors and their families as well as the church.

As my thoughts turned once again to the life of Samson, I came to the realization that although his life was marred by pride, foolish choices and compromise, this story is not about him. Rather it is the story about God and his faithful purpose for the nation of Israel. God's overall purposes did not falter because of the failure and disobedience of Samson. God still used Samson's impulsive actions, personal agendas and vendettas to gain victory for the nation of Israel. He continued to use him to mete out his judgment against the Philistines and in doing so a measure of freedom was gained for Israel. However, I am quite certain that Samson could have led with far greater effectiveness. He could have accomplished greater feats for the people he was called to both lead and serve. I believe the nation of Israel could have gained greater freedom had Samson's life been fully submitted to God.

I have also come to the realization just as God continued to work through Samson, with all his short comings, he will continue his work through the children of Samson and Delilah who lead our churches today. God remains faithful to his word and his purposes. He does not remove his call and gifting from his servants, even when they implement their own visions or build their own empires and bring great harm to others. Remarkably, God uses leaders despite their pride, impure motives and ungodly behavior. His will and purposes are not unraveled through their disobedience. He does not wring his hands in despair when they fall short. I've learned God is very slow to get angry. He does not often mete out his judgment quickly and seldom do we witness overt acts of judgment or discipline. However, although we may not witness the overt judgment of God, I am convinced that he does not ignore sin whether it is great or small. I believe when we live self absorbed and prideful lives, when we build our own empires and bring harm to others, God allows leanness of soul to set in. We can live in pretense for a very long time, but eventually our true character and spiritual condition will be exposed.

God called Samson, not only to be a spiritual leader for Israel, but to lead the nation in gaining freedom from foreign and oppressing nations. It was a high call, but in the end, Samson's ministry and life ended through his own sin and foolishness. And just as Samson's behavior caught up with him in the end, so too, I believe the sinful and compromising behavior of the children of Samson and Delilah will eventually be their downfall.

Chapter 4

LIVING IN THE CONSEQUENCES

The swords of criticism and accusation fell silent! Words of love and appreciation were being expressed. It was our farewell lunch. But it was neither a celebration of the past nor was it a hopeful look to the future. I believe it was tense, awkward and uncomfortable for most of us. Thankfully it was now over! For me there was a grief stricken sigh of relief. We were finally able to draw the curtains and take refuge. I no longer had to listen or focus on the accusations and criticisms. It was time to regroup. It was time to take stock. And it was only now that we were able to contemplate our future. Although we were facing a time of uncertainty and pain, there were decisions that had to be made and plans which needed to be implemented. For awhile each day brought with it new realities and new consequences. Those initial days, weeks and even months felt as though I was constantly being slapped in the face; each day a stinging reminder of the damage that had been done. I found myself struggling to find my balance and footing. I lived in hope that life would once again return to normal, but as the months and even years went by I realized that although life goes on, we were living a new normal.

We faced many difficult and unwanted consequences after we left the church and it would be easy to simply churn out a petty list of complaints. But churning out a list of grievances would not be helpful. It would just be fuel for anger and open the door to bitterness and the desire for revenge. Instead, I have chosen to take a look at some of the consequences my family and, more specifically, I faced and the impact they had on my life. I will share the many truths the Lord taught me as I struggled to live in those consequences and was finally able to come to places of acceptance and find healing. There is also, another major consequence I have not discussed in this chapter: Post Traumatic Stress Disorder. I felt there was enough which needed to be said on this topic that it warranted its own chapter.

Financial:

The first and most likely major consequence of anyone losing their job is financial. And the first of many questions that will need to be asked is how will we survive? Job loss brings great uncertainty in life. There is no way to know how long you may be unemployed and therefore steps need to be taken which will enable financial survival without an income for a time. We were very fortunate to receive a severance package that allowed us extra time to make the necessary changes. But if little or no severance package is offered, it makes the financial consequences all the more serious and difficult. Although some may believe a severance package is given to avoid a lawsuit that is simply not the case. A severance package is also not a parting gift nor it is money paid in appreciation for time served. Although it is not always a legal requirement, it is the obligation of the employer to his employee when that employee is terminated. It is money paid as compensation, based on the length of service, to that employee.

One aspect of the financial situation we now found ourselves in was that we had to give consideration to our health and dental plans, our pension plans and life insurance policies. These had been in place through the church and so at our termination many of these benefits came to an end. We had to give careful consideration whether or not we could personally pick up the financial burden to maintain some or all of the benefits previously held. The monetary value of a benefit package may be considerable. It may in fact be a large portion of one's salary and losing them can therefore be a substantial loss.

Another huge financial factor was our home. When leaving a church, most pastors will face a move. There is almost no way to get around it. In smaller communities there are just not enough churches available to make it viable to remain. In large metropolitan areas commuting long distances between your home and the new church is likely not an option. In either case, it is wise to prepare for the eventuality of a move. We lived in a large metropolitan area and owned our home. The question of whether or not to sell our home began early on. In fact, the preparation to sell our home began before we even left the church. We chose to sell and rent while we waited for a new position to become available. This was a difficult decision; one made somewhat blindly, with huge financial implications but in the end, for us, it was a wise choice.

The reality of leaving a church under difficult or controversial circumstances is that some members of your family may not be able to enter a church let alone be part of ministering in one. As a pastor, consideration will have to be given whether your career may be over. Whether that is a temporary or permanent state will clarify itself with time. But at some point, the question may need to be asked as to what you will do if you or members of your family are through with ministry. Will you retrain? If so, what costs will you incur? Should you find a temporary job with the hope that enough healing will take place so you can return to the pastorate at a later time? Although, for a long time, I found even entering a church extremely difficult, I never considered that our time in ministry was over. I do not have an answer as to why that was the case. I just always felt that one day I would heal enough to make it possible for us to return.

Perhaps another financial consequence to consider, albeit optional, is the cost of professional counseling. Many pastors and their families, who leave their churches under difficult circumstances, are devastated. They are in need of professional care but can ill afford it. Fortunately a counselor can sometimes be found who will offer their services for free. Sometimes the denomination you are affiliated with may also offer free counseling services. But if free is not available, you may face hundreds if not thousands of dollars in fees. Although it is difficult to consider incurring that extra cost, especially if you are already facing financial hardship, I would highly recommend making the sacrifice. I found my own experience with counseling extremely beneficial and necessary. I needed the insight of a trained counselor to understand what I was suffering from. I needed their wisdom to move me forward in my healing. Thankfully my counselor was generous, offering his services for free, but accepted the very small amount we chose to pay.

LOSS OF FRIENDS AND BROKEN RELATIONSHIPS:

Much of our lives revolved around the church and when we left we suddenly found ourselves cut off from people we had known for years. It is natural for some friends to continue their support of you even after you have left the church, but unfortunately those friendships can become a continuum for further division. With that in mind we chose to greatly limit our contact with former church members. When we did meet, we carefully guarded our conversations in order not to stimulate further division in the church. But not being a part of the church family left us feeling a huge sense of isolation and loneliness.

To date we remain in touch with some people, but there are other friendships which have not survived. Because some friendships never move beyond a superficial level, during times of testing, you simply go your separate ways with little or no repercussions. But when close friends wound us, it is more difficult to simply move on. I felt deeply wounded by loved and trusted friends. I believed our friendship was deep enough to survive testing. It was not. As a result, I have become what I call, a reluctant friend. That is to say, engaging in relationships now seems far more risky. I feel a little gun shy. My church experience has taught me how rare it is to have a trusted and devoted friend and how difficult it is to be that friend to others. I now question whether my current friends would remain faithful, loyal or devoted should our relationship be tested. I no longer trust or presume our friendship would survive. I realize that I no longer want to risk the pain friendship may demand. I have become wary of intimate friendships and somewhat weary of the effort of friendship. For now, it just seems wise to carefully weigh the implications before jumping into new relationships and deepening old ones.

As I have reflected on the matter of friendship, I've realized that because I've experienced personal broken relationships within the church, my relationship with the Church as a whole is also damaged. I have lost a measure of trust in the Church. It no longer feels as safe as it once did. I also have to admit to the fact that if my husband was not a pastor, I would probably not make a great effort to go to church every Sunday. Being wounded by the Church can become a great excuse to find other things to do.

LOSS OF REPUTATION:

"Choose a good reputation over great riches, for being held in high esteem is better than having silver or gold" (Proverbs 22:1).

"A good reputation is more valuable than the most expensive perfume" (Ecclesiastes 7:1).

When one is publically criticized and accusations are leveled, reputations will be tarnished and damaged. The gravity of the criticisms or accusations will have a bearing on how permanent the damage will be. There can be enough damage done to affect just how quickly a new pastoral position is found. Our reputations were damaged even among our greatest supporters. To this day I believe there are those who think less of us because of the criticism brought during the final months of our tenure. Although I cannot accurately judge the degree to which we were impacted, I believe the criticism and accusations had some effect on our ability to find a new position. As the months turned into years, and we still did not have a permanent position, it became harder to face the question of have you found a new church yet? Although this question was asked out of genuine concern for us, it began to feel awkward and uncomfortable. In the years we searched for a permanent position some churches turned us down while other times we were the ones who said no. Although it may seem foolish to have turned down churches that were pursuing us, we felt quite certain that the Lord had asked this of us. We felt that we could not allow the pressure of passing time to force us to take just any opportunity that came along. We felt very strongly that we needed to allow the Lord to direct us to the church he wanted us to serve no matter how long the wait or how foolish we looked.

Sometimes we have earned a bad reputation, other times our name is discredited without cause. But regardless of how our reputations become tarnished, they can be rebuilt. Credibility is not a onetime event; rather it is forged throughout a lifetime. Thankfully, we have been given the gift of time to build, or if needed, to re-build our reputations.

Rumors:

I was very surprised, when in the initial stages of talking with a church my husband had sent his resume to, they asked him about the lawsuit we had filed against our former church. As it happened, one of their members was related to someone in our former church and this was the information they had passed on. We were able to assure the search committee we had not threatened or initiated any legal action against our former church. We also directed them to the conference minister for further clarification and validation. Thankfully this church did follow through with our suggestion and later called to confirm what we had told them was indeed the truth. It is important to understand that because a pastor is given a severance package does not mean he has threatened a law suit. Although this situation may seem a little humorous, it is not. No credible church is going to call a pastor who has sued their former church. I also wonder what would have happened if those on the search committee hadn't had the courage to outright ask us whether we had pursued a lawsuit. What if they had never made the effort to verify our statement? Certainly a black mark would have remained over our name and our reputations would have remained tarnished in their minds. I am sure we are not the only ones who have had this experience and therefore I find myself asking the question, how many churches simply dismiss resumes because they have heard a rumor and believe a lie. Although I found myself a little frustrated that someone found it necessary to misspeak, I recognized rumors to be just another consequence we had to face and put behind us.

SPIRITUAL CONSEQUENCES:

Division within the church not only affects numbers, trust and unity, but it has spiritual consequences as well. Division affects both individuals and the church body as a whole. I am aware of a few individuals who, because of what took place at their church, found going to church very difficult and others who no longer attend church at all. I also know of some who questioned their relationship with the Lord because of what they had witnessed. Perhaps a more accurate statement would be that they questioned their relationship with the church, which in turn has affected their relationship with God.

For me personally, although confused, angry and sitting in a lot of muck and mire, I believe my spiritual life continued to grow and even flourish. I was never angry or embittered toward the Lord for allowing such deep wounding. Instead, I found the Lord to be my friend, my confidant and my refuge. I did a lot of praying during this time and gratefully, the Lord did a lot of listening. I felt complete freedom to tell him exactly what I thought about those who brought harm to me and my family. I complained an awful lot, but I also allowed the Lord to search my heart. I probably did as much confessing as complaining. I did not cherish sin in my heart. And I never once felt the Lord's disapproval even while thinking and saying some very unkind things about those who brought so much harm. I always felt thoroughly loved and accepted by the Lord. He knew I needed a sounding board. I needed to have the freedom to speak honestly about how I saw things and how I felt. For me, praying was a way to work through the anger and pain. Although I spent a great deal of time confessing my sins, I did not have instant victory over them. But the first step to that victory was to be in agreement with the Lord as to the reality of my heart condition.

Although I was never angry with the Lord, there is a rather surprising, or perhaps strange consequence I did experience. For a time, I had to avoid reading certain books of the Bible because they aroused deep feelings of anger and resentment against those who harmed me. They incited in me the desire to even the score. Psalms just happens to be one of those books. Perhaps reading Psalm 35 would help you understand what I mean.

Psalm 35

O Lord, oppose those who oppose me.
Declare war on those who are attacking me.
Put on your armor, and take up your shield.
Prepare for battle, and come to my aid.
Lift up your spear and javelin and block the way of my enemies.
Let me hear you say, "I am your salvation!"

Humiliate and disgrace those trying to kill me;

turn them back in confusion.
Blow them away like chaff in the wind – a wind sent by the angel of the Lord.
Make their path dark and slippery, with the angel of the Lord pursuing them.
Although I did them no wrong, they laid a trap for me.
Although I did them no wrong, they dug a pit for me.
So let sudden ruin overtake them!
Let them be caught in the snare they set for me!
Let them fall to destruction in the pit they dug for me.

Then I will rejoice in the Lord.
I will be glad because he rescues me.
I will praise him from the bottom of my heart:
"Lord, who can compare with you?
Who else rescues the weak and helpless from the strong?
Who else protects the poor and needy from those who want to rob them?"

Malicious witnesses testify against me.
They accuse me of things I don't even know about.
They repay me with evil for the good I do.
I am sick with despair.
Yet when they were ill, I grieved for them.
I even fasted and prayed for them, but my prayers returned unanswered.
I was sad, as though they were my friends or family,
as if I were grieving for my own mother.
But they are glad now that I am in trouble;
they gleefully join together against me.
I am attacked by people I don't even know;
they hurl slander at me continually.
They mock me with the worst kind of profanity, and they snarl at me.

How long, O Lord, will you look on and do nothing?
Rescue me from their fierce attacks.
Protect my life from these lions!
Then I will thank you in front of the entire congregation.

I will praise you before all the people.

Don't let my treacherous enemies rejoice over my defeat.
Don't let those who hate me without cause gloat over my sorrow.
They don't talk of peace;
they plot against innocent people who are minding their own business.
They shout that they have seen me doing wrong.
"Aha," they say. "Aha!" With our own eyes we saw him do it!"

O Lord, you know all about this. Do not stay silent.
Don't abandon me now, O Lord. Wake up! Rise to my defense!
Take up my case, my God and my Lord.
Declare me "not guilty," O Lord my God, for you give me justice.
Don't let my enemies laugh about me in my troubles.
Don't let them say, "Look! We have what we wanted!
Now we will eat him alive!"

May those who rejoice at my troubles be humiliated and disgraced.
May those who triumph over me be covered with shame and dishonor.

But give great joy to those who have stood with me in my defense.
Let them continually say, "Great is the Lord, who enjoys helping his servant."
Then I will tell everyone of your justice and goodness,
and I will praise you all day long.

Although I love the Psalms, I found some chapters stirring up my emotions to the degree of wanting revenge. I felt they were hindering my progress to forgive. I therefore chose to limit my time in the Psalms until I was well enough not to be emotionally charged by them.

Physical Consequences:

I believe what happens to us emotionally, eventually affects us physically. When individuals face an extended time of stress, they will most certainly experience physical symptoms of some kind or another. Some may struggle to sleep and will find sleep aids beneficial to get them through a difficult time. Some will eat their way through the stress, while others lose their appetite and will eat little. Some may experience depression, anxiety attacks and ulcers. Emotional stress can bring on any number of physical symptoms.

I did not suffer greatly from physical symptoms, but there was no doubt, I was stressed. Suffering noticeable weight loss was really the only obvious physical symptom I had. However, several months into our ordeal, my husband returned from a particularly intimidating meeting. He informed me that at that meeting the criticism had turned to me and grave concerns had been expressed. So great were these concerns that the leadership felt my husband's credentials as a pastor should be revoked. My husband's call in life and career was now in jeopardy. The Lord had forewarned us that the criticism leveled against me would ultimately have a bearing on my husband. These very words were being fulfilled that evening. I was absolutely stunned! I was shocked by the accusations and amazed by how far some would go to ensure my husband's resignation. I remember praying that night, bringing this new development before the Lord, and I soon fell into a deep and sound sleep. But hours later I was suddenly awakened. My whole body was trembling uncontrollably. I had not awakened in fear and I was not in a state of panic. I was just shaking. It was then I realized the toll the last few months had taken on my body. I remember wondering if my body had gone into shock. But as I shook, my thoughts turned once again to the Lord and I began praying. The trembling stopped and I once again fell into a deep and peaceful sleep. It never happened again.

I am very thankful that I never had difficulty sleeping during this ordeal. I did not lie awake for hours on end. I did not wring my hands in worry, though our plight was never far from my mind. I believe there are two reasons for this. First, I felt my conscience was clear. Although I came under intense scrutiny and accusations were made, I knew what I was being accused of had been twisted and embellished to serve an agenda. That is not to say there were not seeds of truth in what was being said, but it was far from accurate. Secondly, my evenings were and are generally spent in the word and in prayer. I simply brought everything before the Lord. He was my shield, my refuge, my safety, my sanity, and my peace; especially during this time. We desperately need to be people of prayer. When we are wounded, our prayers are a way which allows the Lord to work out his healing in us. We need to approach his throne with boldness. And after we've poured out our hearts to the Lord, we need to stop and listen to what he may want to say to us. He desires to share his wisdom with us. He has counsel to give us. He has truth and healing to bring us. He desires to fill us with hope and his peace.

Mistrust:

After we left the church I felt very lonely and isolated. But the flip side of this coin is, I also developed a very great and desperate need for privacy. I found it very difficult to open myself up to others, especially new people. This became glaringly obvious when my husband signed up for Facebook. I checked our email the next day and at least twenty people were requesting to be our friends. I found myself in tears and panicked even though most friend requests were family members. I felt angry and frightened. I did not want any information about me or my family on a public domain. I had grave concerns just how the most innocent information might be interpreted and used to bring further harm to us. Thankfully, my husband only signed up for Facebook; he never actually checks it or posts anything on it. This is a great relief to me!

I also found myself constantly shushing my husband. I cringed every time he took the phone outside and had conversations for all the neighbors to hear. When I felt he was giving out more information than necessary, I would glare at him or nudge him in an effort to stop the flow of details coming from him. It didn't matter how innocent the information, I wanted complete silence and secrecy as far as my family was concerned.

In this desperate need for privacy I built a very thick and very high wall of self protection. I believe my need for privacy is based in mistrust and that mistrust stems from feeling betrayed. Even today, I feel its sting. And yet now, as I write this book, I feel as though I am betraying myself for I am the one revealing intimate details of my life. Frankly, I do not want those who have brought harm to know the extent of damage that has been inflicted. I do not want them to acquire any information about my life or gain any insight into what I have had to work through. I do not want them to gain further knowledge about me or my family. In my mind they have taken enough, and I do not want to give them one more piece of me; not one more shred of information regarding my life or my family's! At some level, I fear further reprisals from them. I certainly do not want to provide further ammunition that might be used against my family. I feel vulnerable and a little afraid. And so as I write both the tears and the adrenalin begin to flow. There is a huge part of me that wants to go into hiding; to keep the walls of silence and self-protection standing tall. But I understand that hiding behind walls of self-protection only act to rob me of abundance in life. Walls rob me of forming new friendships and moving forward in life with joy. Walls rob me of finding healing and sharing my life with others. Although I am now less vigilant in my extreme efforts to remain private and obscure, I wonder if to a certain extent, this will be a permanent state of mind.

ENDLESS CONVERSATIONS AND SPEECHES:

One of the most persistent and difficult consequences I have had to deal with is the many, many conversations that I've had, and the many speeches I have given. I have held court, non-stop, for months and yes, even years. I have relentlessly and thoroughly prepared my defense. I have fearlessly and incessantly argued my case. I have amazed my enemies with my eloquence. I have demolished them with my brilliance! I have put them to shame with my sharp tongue and quick wit. I have made them tremble with my stinging arguments and unhinged them with my powerful line of reasoning. But the fact is not one of the thousands of speeches was ever delivered. No one has been amazed by my debating skills. I have convinced no one of their wrong doing. I have gained no justice for myself. The reason is simply because every speech given and every conversation held was in my mind. I alone sat in the courtroom! I alone heard the arguments! I alone pronounced the fair and just judgment that those who harmed me so richly deserved.

So pervasive were my conversations and speeches that some nights my dreams became an arena for them. I would awaken with my soul in anguish. These night time courtroom proceedings would stir up my emotions so that my mind would grind out speeches throughout the following day. Unfortunately I found no peace in these one sided conversations. It was an endless and fruitless exercise. It was an inescapable quagmire. It was emotionally very tiring, but there just did not seem to be an off switch for my mind. I felt as though if I could somehow just say the right words; if I could say it perfectly I would finally be heard. People would finally see the error of their ways and I would get the justice I both desired and deserved. Although I desperately sought justice from the court held in my mind, I was simply powerless to obtain it for myself.

I think the Lord must have been tired of hearing the endless rhetoric as well because one day he quietly said, *this is not an oasis*. I knew in an instant what he meant! The speeches and the endless conversations were not an oasis. An oasis is a place to rest. It is a place where there is shade, food and water. It is a place of hope and safety. And it is a place of life amidst a barren wasteland. Endless speeches and conversations offered no shade, no food, no water, no hope, no peace and no rest. No life is found there. It is a barren and forsaken place, and to stay in that place of endless repeating conversations was to finally choose death.

I knew that I could no longer allow the speeches to control me. I was painfully aware and angry with myself for wasting so much of my time thinking about those who brought harm. I am sure they were not losing any sleep over my situation or over what they had done. And so I acknowledged to the Lord that I was in a wasteland that led to death. I wanted life. I knew in him was life. He is the oasis! He is the bread of heaven and the living water. He is rest, peace, freedom, hope and deliverance. Ultimately he alone can give justice. I have had to work hard "to take every thought captive to the obedience of Christ" (2 Corinthians 10:12, NASB). It has been a painfully slow process and I still have to work hard because there are days where I fall into the trap of making speeches all over again. But I quickly recognize that I cannot find rest there; there is no life in that place. I cannot change one thing by my many speeches. This court cannot and will never give me justice.

Depression:

Although one would think that depression would be an obvious consequence to being profoundly wounded, I found I did not struggle with it. I am incredibly grateful for that mercy. Although I experienced some dark days and yes, even depressing days, I never found myself living under a black cloud. I was never in a place of being unable to get out of bed or barely able to function. Throughout this time I experienced great joy, laughter and fun. Our family has celebrated graduations and new jobs. We had an engagement to celebrate and a wedding to plan. We celebrated with our children as they purchased their own homes. We became grandparents! My husband and I have taken an older home and extensively renovated it; this being a great love of mine and very rewarding. We have traveled quite extensively. We have carried on working. And I am writing; this alone is a remarkable feat.

Although I have not found myself struggling with depression, I believe that I have gone through an extended time of great sadness, grief and deep mourning. We've lost much and it takes time to come to terms with that loss. It takes time to grieve. It takes time to mourn. It takes time to rebuild one's life after a life altering experience. It takes time to gain balance and perspective. It takes time to find your new normal. It takes time to find and live in vibrancy and joy again. Grief is a part of normal life experience and we need to acknowledge and even embrace it. We are wise to grieve well; taking all the time needed without feeling embarrassed or feeling like we need apologize for our tears.

I would simply add, as strange as this may sound, I feel as though I have had long moments of joyful abundance amidst the sorrow and deep pain.

SUICIDE:

Thoughts of suicide can also be a very real consequence when deeply wounded. I felt the fiery darts of the enemy telling me that my family would be better off if I was dead. I also heard the enemy tell me my death would serve as punishment to those who wounded me. I recognized these thoughts immediately as coming from the pit of hell. They were lies and I quickly took them captive. The truth is my family was not better off if I was dead. My death would only have added to their suffering. And as for my death serving as punishment for those who wounded me, the truth is, my death would neither have punished them nor would it have convicted them of their wrong doing. Instead, some might have thought that being overcome by guilt I took my own life. And quite frankly, I was not about to make that a reality!

GRUDGES, BITTERNESS AND ANGER:

It was nearing the end of our time at the church. I remember sitting in the living room of friends. They were trying to encourage us but also speak truthfully to some of the concerns that had surfaced during the last months of our tenure. As the evening progressed they began to speak very specifically to the issues relating to me. They listed off numerous grievances they and others in the church had. I just sat quietly. I did not respond to their concerns or accusations. My reason for doing so was twofold. First I felt so overwhelmed with what we had endured over the previous months I had no desire, no ability and no energy to argue my case. Secondly, our friends never once asked me to respond, clarify or refute anything they had just said. I can only assume they honestly believed they had accurate information and credible accounts and therefore needed no input from me. But what really perturbed me was they really had no firsthand knowledge of the matters they were raising. All their concerns and grievances came from second, if not third and fourth hand information. How could they be so sure they had accurate information?

The accusations that had been made were serious and yet I was never asked to explain myself. Why didn't anyone want to have my account? I felt ignored. I felt misjudged and maligned. I can't tell you how incredibly angry this made me. This ate at me! I constantly came before the Lord and poured out my heart to him. I was in anguish over what had been said and done. I was angry that one or two people could twist the truth and others couldn't see through their schemes. I was angry that people got caught up in the gossip and hearsay. I was livid that embellished and false accusations had been made against me. I could not let it go. My prayers had had the same ring to them for months. I declared to the Lord that I had been misjudged and that it was unjust. I felt robbed! I felt betrayed, shamed and humiliated! I was angry! At long last, I had to acknowledge I was holding grudges. Finally one evening as I prayed, I cried out, "Oh Lord, I just felt so *powerless* when…!" And then suddenly, as if a light had been turned on, I understood! The Lord began to show me that all grudges are based in a sense of *powerlessness*. A grudge that is held is perceived power over a person or situation. It is a way for an individual to regain power over that which was taken away. It is the means to re-establish an individual's rights and take back what one feels is owed. Unfortunately this power is only in your mind. It is not real power.

With this new understanding I began to pour out my heart before the Lord once again. A long litany of grief spilled out as I recounted the specific ways in which I felt powerless. I felt powerless when the pursuit to discredit my family and our ministry began. I felt powerless as a long list of criticism was publicly made against my husband. I felt powerless over those who tried to humiliate and disgrace him. I felt powerless over those who tarnished our reputations. I felt powerless when I discovered how much gossip had gone on; how much had been said behind our backs. I felt powerless as people judged us on inaccurate and flawed information. I felt powerless to defend myself against terrible accusations. I felt powerless when no one asked to hear my side of the story. I felt powerless when intimate information entrusted to dearest friends was openly shared with others. I felt powerless when those friends betrayed me. I felt powerless by their ambush. I felt powerless that I could not fully disclose certain facts because to do so would betray the confidences of the very ones who betrayed mine. I felt powerless over those whose sin and deception was now heaped on me. I felt powerless as the blame for their actions was squarely placed on my shoulders. I felt powerless to save my husband's career which was now in jeopardy. I felt powerless when I had to go before an adjudicating board so they could judge whether or not my husband would retain his credentials as a pastor. I felt powerless and humiliated when I had to explain to them intimate and confidential details of my life; details which were never meant for public knowledge and scrutiny. I felt powerless to protect my family from the consequences of a church process run amuck. I felt powerless to bring any consequences to those who twisted the truth.

I felt powerless over those who manipulated the church. I felt powerless over our future. Oh, so completely and utterly powerless!

As I prayed I felt the anger and anguish yet again; the tears flowed freely. I finally recognized and understood my feelings of utter powerlessness. I understood that it is soul piercing to be so utterly and completely stripped of power. I understood why and how grudges begin. But I also understood there is no real power held over a person or situation because a grudge is only held in one's mind and heart. Holding a grudge resolves nothing. You will not and cannot regain any power through it. It cannot bring truth or healing. It cannot bring freedom. You remain powerless to change the circumstances or force someone to give back what they have taken or what you feel they owe. Continuing to hold a grudge will only eat further away at your soul cultivating anger and resentment, self-pity, bitterness and the desire for revenge. Holding grudges keeps you living in self-pity and clouds your judgment. And self-pity keeps you living without hope because you are constantly looking to the past. But the past is just that; it is the past! It cannot be undone and it cannot be changed. We can only learn from it and then move on.

I remember driving in the car one day talking to the Lord about our situation. I was quietly listening for his wisdom when he said to me: "do not open the guest room door to bitterness." As I reflected on this I realized that though a grudge grows out of feeling powerless, I was the one who held the power over bitterness. The choice was mine whether or not I would open the door. Just as a house guest must follow certain protocol such as being invited or given permission to enter in, so too, bitterness must follow the same rules. Unfortunately I believe that the guest room for bitterness is always prepared. It is always ready for occupancy with clean sheets, chocolates on the pillows and fresh towels folded like swans at the end of the bed. Bitterness is a sneaky, persistent foe that constantly knocks at the door of your heart with promises of comfort and friendship. Bitterness sees the injustice suffered and says, Look at what they've done to you! I would never do that! I'll never betray you! It whispers sweet nothings in your ear. And because your damaged heart, your pierced soul, is desperately seeking comfort and affirmation, it is easily tricked into opening that door. But the truth is, once through the door, bitterness is a terrible guest with deep and damaging roots. It is a demanding and angry guest driving others away. It is a most difficult guest to get rid of.

We must make every effort to keep the door to bitterness locked. I have worked hard to do just that. I do not feel embittered, but to this day I am angry that I was misjudged and treated unjustly. I believe we should be angry when there is gossip, lies and betrayal. We should be angry when we see others denigrated and humiliated. We should be angry when people's reputations are tarnished and careers are ended through disparaging remarks and hasty judgments. We should be angry at injustice. Anger is the correct and normal response to something that is wrong. It is the correct and normal response to an injustice committed. Although anger can be healthy and a correct response, we need to recognize how quickly it can cross the line and become unhealthy. It can begin to control us. We need to be aware that the flames of anger are unquenchable and that holding grudges and living in bitterness only serves to fuel that anger. I continually acknowledged my anger before the Lord. I did not want my life ruled by it and I did not want to give Satan a foothold through that anger. Although it was difficult not to continually feed this fire I was careful not to allow anger to control me.

The Blame Game:

The choices we make in life will always carry with them consequences whether for good or bad. It is hard enough to live with consequences which may result from our own foolishness, but harder to face are the consequences brought on through the harmful actions of others. We, who are deeply wounded, may find ourselves in a place of great anger and resentment. Anger makes us vulnerable to having an exaggerated or slanted perception of what took place. And because our perspective may be skewed, we may find ourselves susceptible to misplace or inflate blame; to impugn others unjustly. It becomes all too easy to blame others for every consequence we have endured. I found it difficult to not vilify those I felt pierced my soul. I could not separate their hurtful actions from the friendship once shared or the good work they had accomplished for the church. I had and still have to carefully guard myself against playing the blame game. Playing this game is not unlike playing the game of Pin the Tail on the Donkey. Just as we can rarely pin the donkey's tail in its correct position while wearing a blindfold, so too, when we are blinded by anger, bitterness or resentment, we cannot accurately see who to pin the blame on. We can't always see clearly enough to know who to blame or how much they are to blame for the harm brought to us. The truth is those who pierced my soul do not bear the responsibility for every consequence I experienced. Yes, their actions were harmful and many of the consequences are in fact the direct result of their behavior. And yes, their actions precipitated a domino effect of damage, but to put the blame in its entirety on those who harmed me would be excessive and unjust. Thankfully, my family and a few really great friends walked through this time with me. I needed to confide in them. They protected me, encouraged me and prayed with me. Where my perception was skewed they helped me find balance. They kept me grounded in the truth.

REVENGE:

When we have been harmed, I believe there is always a desire for justice. However, though we may think we only wanted justice, I believe more often than not, our human heart desires revenge. Justice is to receive what one deserves whether that is for good done or for misdeeds. Revenge is the desire to do something in retaliation for a misdeed. It is a desire to bring punishment to a person for their wrong doing. When we experience deep wounding at the hands of another we may take up the sword of revenge. For a time I hated those who brought so much harm. I hated what they did and even more, I hated that they did not see the damage done. I wanted those who harmed me to be held accountable for their actions. And so finally, I had to ask myself the question whether I had taken up a sword of revenge. Did I really only desire justice or was I in fact hungering for revenge? When I was truly honest with myself, I had to admit that as much as I thought I wanted justice I have really desired those who harmed me to be punished. Yes, I did want revenge. I wanted payback! I wanted them to, in some way, experience failure in their lives so that I could gloat over them. My daughter has offered to take me on drive-by-eggings. I have not yet taken her up on that offer, although, at times I have been tempted. Even today I think it might feel really, really good! But if I am truly honest with myself, simply egging houses is not enough. I want those who had brought so much harm and suffering, to suffer even more than I did. The punishment I would really like to inflict is worse than what was done to me. I believe that is the heart of revenge; do worse unto others than was done to you. Revenge follows the law of escalation and it is therefore a dangerous thing in human hands. Vengeance belongs to the Lord. There is no room for revenge in our hearts. I believe it is for exactly these reasons that scripture warns us not to seek vengeance but to allow the Lord to handle the matter. When we take actions in revenge, I believe we end up committing a greater sin than was trespassed against us. And so I had to renounce my desire for payback; for revenge. I needed not only to sheathe that sword of revenge but give it back to the Lord. I needed to acknowledge that vengeance belonged to the Lord and that he could be trusted to ultimately bring justice.

SHAME:

We entrust our souls to others with the belief that our soul will not be harmed. But when trust is broken, shame can be the result. I have finally come to the realization that for a very, very long time I have felt shame over our church exit. I felt shamed in the way we were evaluated and judged. I felt shamed by the criticisms and accusations made against both my husband and me. I felt shamed when I heard of the secret meetings that were held only to find greater fault and cast further blame. And I felt shame as the months turned into years and we still had not accepted a new pastoral position.

Although I was always aware of the embarrassment and shame I felt, it is only recently, as I have begun to memorize and meditate on Psalms 34 that the realization of my shame has come more sharply into focus. Psalm 34:5 says, "Those who look to the Lord for help will be radiant with joy; *no shadow of shame will darken their faces*." Instead of being radiant with joy, shame darkens our soul. It eats into our soul. It erodes our self-worth and our confidence. It robs us of dignity and self-esteem. Shame, like a shadow, casts a net of self-doubt and hopelessness over our lives.

I believe we have all said or done things that we are ashamed of. We need to grieve and sorrow over our sins. We need to repent. But sometimes we feel shame through no fault of our own. Shame comes to us through the sins of others. Whether the sin is ours or the sins of others against us, shame often remains on us like a residue or as scripture calls it, a shadow. We allow shame to darken our faces when the Lord invites us to come to him for help. I have realized that when we feel shame we instinctively lower our faces; eyes to the ground. But when we look to the Lord, he cups his hand under our chin and gently lifts our face to his. He looks us straight in the eyes. And as our face is lifted high to meet his gaze, there is no disappointment or condemnation in his eyes. There are no shaming words spoken over us.

I believe that I am still in the process of overcoming my shame. I believe much of our self-worth is molded and shaped through the eyes of others. They are a mirror of acceptance or rejection. I have found it most difficult to hold my head high when others drove it down through their criticism, accusations and condemnation; through their rejection. Healing for me has included allowing the Lord to lift my head again. And as he has washed the shame off of my face, he has become my mirror. He is the correct reflection of who I am. What finally matters is what he knows and thinks about me, not what others think they know or what they have said. And so I choose to bask in the Lord's grace and mercy, in his forgiveness and acceptance, in his hope and peace. I am therefore, radiant with joy!

Chapter 5

Post Traumatic Stress

One day someone I had a close friendship with, came into my place of employment. During the process of evaluating our tenure, they had taken some actions, which left me feeling baffled and deeply hurt. I had no contact with this individual for more than two years and was therefore taken completely by surprise when they came up behind me and cheerfully greeted me. Although my back was turned, I instantly recognized the voice! The adrenalin began flowing and my hands began to shake. I believe I turned to face this person. I also believe I said something to them, but then I suddenly found myself alone. I had simply turned my back on this individual and walked away. But I have absolutely no memory of doing so. I do not know how I arrived in the location where I now stood, shaking uncontrollably. I am also not sure who was more surprised, me or the individual I had just left standing there. Please understand, there was no malice on my part. I had not intended to snub or act rudely towards this individual. I had not decided it was payback time. My behavior was on a purely emotional level; a knee jerk reaction if you will. I did not think! I ran! And as I stood there shaking, now quite aware and shocked by what I had just done, I remember the Lord quietly and repeatedly saying, *I can use all things for good.* Those words brought a measure of calmness to me and I was able to refocus and return to work.

Incredibly, this was not the first time this individual surprised me at work. The first time was almost two years earlier and only a few months after we left the church. I remember the exact date. I remember what I was doing and what I was wearing. I even remember that I was having a good hair day! This day is etched in my memory. I was at work and this individual was suddenly standing in front me. I wanted to run but several factors came into play and I simply could not escape them. My heart began pounding so fast I could hardly catch my breath. My hands shook violently. I tried hard to concentrate on my work, all the while they just kept chatting, completely oblivious to my distress. All I could do was avoid making eye contact and try to answer their questions as civilly and briefly as humanly possible. And then came their parting words! "I am praying for you!" At that point I almost leapt over the counter and let them have it. Those were fighting words! I wanted to scream at them, "Pray for me! Pray for me! How dare you! How dare you think I would even want you to pray for me! You really have no grip on reality!" I was incensed! It became completely obvious they felt no remorse for their actions which had caused me so much pain. But how could they be so oblivious? Thankfully, I refrained from leaping over the counter. I did not assault them verbally or physically. I think I even managed a good-bye. But I was left reeling and struggled to finish my work that day. I was still shaken days later and it was months before I could think about this incident without the tears and adrenalin flowing.

It was after the second time this individual surprised me at work that I had to acknowledge I was not healing well. This last incident was just the catalyst I needed to return to my counselor. I recognized I was continuing to have significant reactions, both emotionally and physically, to any people or incidents relating to our departure from the church. In fact, I would say my reactions seemed to be getting more severe. I found even the mention of certain people enough to start the adrenalin flowing and my heart pounding. It was unrelenting! My emotions felt just as raw two years after our departure as the day we left. In reality, I would have to say that I was emotionally more unhealthy two years after the fact. I knew I needed help. And so as I sat in my counselor's office we discussed these and other incidents, and my intense reactions to them. My counselor began to talk to me about Post Traumatic Stress Disorder (PTSD). And as we talked I began to understand why my emotions still felt so raw; why I was in such distress and why I was having such intense reactions to relatively minor events.

I certainly lay no claims to be an expert on the subject of PTSD. My knowledge is very much limited to my personal experience. It is my understanding that PTSD is a severe and ongoing emotional reaction to an extreme physical or psychological trauma. It is an anxiety disorder which can develop after exposure to one or more traumatic events that have threatened or caused grave physical harm. It is also caused by profound psychological and emotional trauma, apart from any actual physical harm. Often however, incidents involving both are found to be the cause. PTSD symptoms usually last more than six months and cause significant impairment in social or work relationships and other important areas of functioning. Symptoms may include flashbacks and nightmares; difficulty falling or staying asleep. Individuals will re-experience the traumatic event in some way so that there is an avoidance of places, people, or other things that are a reminder of that event. Symptoms also include persistent and increased arousal or stimulation in the areas of anger or hyper vigilance. Memory may also be affected. The mind will retain some details of the event with pinpoint accuracy while other aspects will simply be blocked out.

Those suffering from PTSD are extremely sensitive to normal life experiences. They will have acute or severe emotional responses to certain events. Specific words or phrases, a person, a sight, a noise or smell, a memory, a subconscious thought or feeling will suddenly propel the emotions of an individual back to the same place or level they felt at the original event or trauma they experienced. These are called *triggers* or *stressors*. When a triggering event occurs, the person suffering from PTSD will react to that event at the same level of emotional intensity as the original trauma, not the triggering event itself. My fleeing the scene after recognizing the voice of a former friend is an example of this. Just *hearing* their voice immediately propelled my emotions to the emotional intensity I felt two years prior. My behavior, though excessive and extreme for what in essence was a casual encounter, was actually a consequence or the result of what had occurred two years earlier.

As my counselor and I continued to talk, he explained to me what I had done was a very normal reaction for someone suffering from PTSD. He helped me understand, when we feel our safety is being threatened, we instinctively take the necessary action to protect ourselves. Although this individual was not a physical threat to me, I still perceived them as a threat, because their actions were a factor in bringing severe consequences to me and my family. In my mind this individual was not safe and fleeing the scene was a very necessary act of self protection. It was normal and even appropriate! I cannot begin to tell you how relieved I was to understand my behavior was normal! This was not an excuse for rude or vengeful behavior, but gave credibility to that behavior. It had not been my intention to be rude or vindictive. I had not lain awake nights plotting my revenge. I had reacted instinctively! I gave no thought to what I did. My feet obeyed my emotions. My counselor's words reassured me and released me from any guilt I had been feeling with regards to what I had done. It is unfortunate that this individual received such an unexpected and strong response from me. Regrettably, they took the brunt for all who wounded me. Without a doubt, my extreme reaction brought confusion and pain to them and for that, I feel badly.

Not everyone suffering from PTSD will react in the same way. Not everyone flees the scene by removing themselves from a perceived threat. Some will flee while others react aggressively and with extreme anger. These responses or reactions are called *fight* or *flight*. When triggered, those who fight will respond with explosive anger; engaging with and confronting anyone caught up in the triggering event. A minor incident will immediately morph into a major event. An individual will react with primal rage without logic or reason. Unfortunately, everyone caught in that triggering event, will be on the receiving end of that rage. Most certainly they will be left shocked and hurt at the excessive anger exhibited over a minor infraction. It is crucial to understand, that outburst of anger really had nothing to do with the triggering event, and everything to do with the original trauma.

On the other hand, those who take the flight stance, run for their lives! They head for the hills. There are no 'in your face' confrontations. The idea is to avoid at all cost. There is a lot of running, hiding and tears. The extreme need to feel safe takes precedence over everything and an individual will go to great lengths to ensure that safety. The anxiety, avoidance and even paranoia exhibited by those who are constantly hiding can be baffling and frustrating to those around them.

Although PTSD may be expressed in different ways, I believe whether you are a fighter or a fleer, anger is a factor. Fighters express their anger, fleers do not; at least not on the primal rage level. I fled, and I was also angry. I simply did not have adequate or appropriate words with which to express the depths of sorrow, the pain and anger in my soul. I believe when a soul has been pierced, for a time emotions are so raw, words either fail or the words gush forth in an unrestrained and vindictive tirade of hatred and blame. For me, spewing hateful words would have served no purpose other than to give more ammunition to those who had already brought harm. When and if I choose to engage with those who pierced my soul, I wish to do so with some dignity and self control.

I would also add, because of the extreme emotional reactions of those suffering with PTSD, they will experience some isolation. It becomes difficult to be around an angry and aggressive person, who not only explodes at minor infractions, but you never know when that anger will be expressed. It is also difficult to be around someone who is in hiding. They are hyper vigilant and paranoid; like a soldier on watch, constantly checking the perimeter for the enemy. But in truth, those suffering from PTSD are, for the most part, unable to act or react differently. I am not saying this to condone or excuse bad behavior. We need to understand that not only are those suffering from PTSD unable to process the trauma they've experienced, they are simply unable to move past it. Just as a broken record plays the same note over and over again, so too, the mind of someone suffering from PTSD gets stuck in the trauma playing the same scene over and over again. They react in the same way over and over again. They cannot move forward. And you cannot heal if you are stuck. You cannot heal if you cannot process the trauma and then move beyond it. If those suffering from PTSD are constantly re-traumatized, they will continue to have disproportionate emotional responses to triggering events. PTSD sufferers are in need of great understanding and compassion. And I believe they are in need of professional help.

We also need to recognize, without exception, trauma involves *loss*. Whether that loss is a loved one, a career, a home, a reputation, innocence, a sense of personal safety, health or anything else for that matter, those suffering PTSD must recognize and come to grips with what it is they have lost. Be it great or small, healing cannot fully come until you have processed that loss and come to a place of forgiveness, acceptance and peace. We have all heard the stories of an individual forgiving another immediately after a tragic event or a crime was committed against them. Although these stories are heartwarming, I wonder if early forgiveness isn't actually premature and even detrimental. I am uncertain if the loss can be processed quickly. I understand the peace that passes all understanding which scripture speaks of, and which rests on someone in times of crisis and tragedy. But I wonder if it is really only as time passes and the full consequences of that loss are felt, that true forgiveness, peace and acceptance can come. This is something I am still reflecting on.

I believe it may take months for PTSD to fully develop. You

do not wake up the day after a traumatic event and have full blown symptoms. I did not know I was suffering from PTSD until I returned to my counselor because I recognized I was still not healing two years after the fact. It may take months, if not years, to recognize you or someone you love is suffering from PTSD. It is important to understand, what will be a traumatic event for one, will not be for another. It is just as important to understand, not everyone will have the full blown symptoms of rage reactions, anxiety, fear or paranoia. PTSD symptoms may take subtle forms of anger, fear, depression or anxiety. We may therefore, not make the connection when we are reacting to something unrelated to the traumatic event we've experienced. We need to be aware of the immense effect trauma has in people's lives. Trauma shapes us. Our lives are molded by the trauma we experience. Untreated, trauma will cast a dark shadow over individuals, with the repercussions of unresolved hurt continually reverberating in their lives. If we cannot heal, this shadow of death will follow us where ever we go. It is unrelenting and unending.

Researchers have created a list of traumatic events that may cause PTSD symptoms to develop. These include violent assault, kidnapping, sexual assault, torture, being held a hostage, a prisoner of war or concentration camp victim, experiencing a disaster, a violent car accident or getting a diagnosis of a life-threatening illness. But there is no mention of being a member of a church or a pastor as a cause of PTSD. I am painfully aware and sobered by the fact that I am indicting the church as causing PTSD in some of their pastors as well as their members. I am in fact stating, the actions of some in our former church caused my PTSD. And the tears begin to flow yet again. To some this may seem to be a ridiculous accusation. But I would counter, I felt attacked and would even say, assaulted by some in the church. It was not a physical attack, but rather an assault of words. Other than noticeable weight loss I showed no signs of this assault, but it felt just as violent as a physical assault. When we were asked to resign and did not immediately do so, an adversarial atmosphere developed very quickly. Everything we did became suspect and any backlash from the congregation was seen as instigated by us. Each week brought with it new criticism and new critics. I felt ambushed by friends. I didn't know where or from whom the next blow was coming. Our reputations were tarnished; our ministry was criticized and our motives were judged. False and grotesque accusations were made. I felt bullied, denigrated and maligned. I felt like prey that was being stalked and hunted. I felt under siege! Church was no longer safe; it was anything but. And it was this sense of feeling under attack which precipitated my PTSD. As difficult as it may be, I believe we need to acknowledge the role a church may play in causing their pastors and their families to suffer from PTSD. Can you imagine if your call and career is to pastor a church, but it is church that triggers you? Is it any wonder so many pastors leave the ministry while others no longer attend church at all?

In its full blown form my PTSD symptoms included being a little paranoid. While driving, I'd watch my review mirror to see whether I was being followed home. I hesitantly opened the blinds because *they* may be parked outside or *they* may drive by. The usual simple and even enjoyable chores like shopping were filled with anxiety. I nervously scanned the store for those familiar faces. I cautiously rounded the corner of the aisles just in case *they* were suddenly there. Strangers who innocently brushed up behind me left me shaken and in tears. While outside of the safety of my home, I lived in perpetual anxiety; the level depending on my chances of running into someone I'd rather not see. The physical and emotional ramifications I experienced, when I had an unexpected or unwanted encounter, were so overwhelming, I tried to avoid any contact at all cost. It has taken days and even weeks to recover from one such incident. I was hyper vigilant; always scanning the crowd for those who may be a threat to my safety. I still do it as it has become an unconscious habit, although it is one that I am trying to break. Strangely enough, even bumping into those who supported us through this time was incredibly difficult for me. I was and to a point, am still on constant high alert when I return to the suburb where this church is located. As of yet, I'm unsure if those who pierced my soul have finished their work because on occasion we hear rumblings of criticism. Although I realize *they* no longer hold any power over me or my family, I still feel threatened. Thankfully, my symptoms have greatly subsided. I have made incredible progress on my journey of healing, but there are still days it is a struggle to remain in a healthy place.

My counselor began to list off the consequences of our departure from the church and then quietly said, "The degree of loss and trauma you have experienced is at the level of parents whose young child has died. You are looking at a minimum of five years of recovery time." FIVE YEARS! I was astounded! I let these words sink in. And then a wave of relief washed over me. I would heal; not today, not even next year, but eventually. The guilt I had felt because I wasn't healing as quickly as I thought I should, or as quickly as others thought I should, was gone in an instant. Hey, I still had a few more years of healing ahead of me! My counselor not only helped me understand the trauma I had gone through, but he gave me permission to be emotionally, mentally and spiritually exactly where I was at. This permission was one of the most, if not the most critical moment of my counseling experience. His acceptance of where I was at, freed me to say no to situations

I knew would trigger me and ultimately hinder my progress. I could say no without guilt. This was incredibly empowering and is what finally enabled me to move forward in my journey of healing. It was at this point my counselor began to work with me to retrain my mind so it did not remain in the proverbial stuck state; like a broken record playing the same note over and over again. When the mind is retrained and able to process the trauma instead of continually living in it, the emotions also begin to respond at normal levels instead of excessive and irrational levels.

Recognizing I was suffering from PTSD also helped my husband understand the extreme emotional distress I was in. He became more empathetic and carefully guarded me; protecting me where he knew I was vulnerable to being unnecessarily triggered. Together we have learned if you push someone who is suffering from PTSD too fast you will only succeed in prolonging their healing process because moving too quickly only traumatizes that individual further. You cannot possibly heal if you are constantly being triggered or re-traumatized.

I have found that even if you are well on your way to recovering, you may find yourself unexpectedly and suddenly triggering. Trauma can and will sneak up on you. The week my husband started pastoring a new church, we painted his office. While we were painting, without thinking, I asked my husband if he remembered the last time we painted his office. He did! As it happened, it was at our former church. At that time we were on a month's leave while the congregation discussed our future. I naively thought since we had this time off, it would be a great opportunity to repaint the office. It had been almost seventeen years since the office had been updated and it was in great need of an overhaul. I thought that either my husband would return to work with his office freshly painted, or a new pastor would reap the benefit of the updates. And so I toiled at scrapping off the wallpaper we had put up almost seventeen years earlier. It was not an easy task. I patched the walls, primed them and then painted them. I even added a decorative shelf. We footed the entire bill. Now as it turned out, painting the office was not the best idea I ever had. In hindsight I would never do it again. What I didn't know was my presence in the office was seen as taking the opportunity to converse with some in the congregation. It was seen as a way to influence and inflame the congregation against those seeking our removal. Motives were attached to my actions, but I was never asked why I had painted. I was never questioned whether, while painting, I had sought people out to *chat* with them. Although I was never confronted or even spoken to, I was accused of inciting the congregation.

And now here I was! It was almost five years later and I was painting my husband's office yet again. The painful accusations came flooding back and immediately my anxiety level went up. I began to fear we had overstepped our bounds in painting this new office. We had not asked for permission to do so. Had we stepped on any toes? What kind of accusations might we now face? And the tears once again flowed. What should have been an exciting new beginning was instead dragging up a painful memory. It revived the trauma. I was triggering again. And it had snuck up on me!

I recognized what was happening and I began to pray. I poured out my pain and my anger that had once again flared up. I acknowledged my fear of being misjudged and attacked once again. I wanted to run from church, every church and never look back. And then the Lord began to speak to me about what happens when we judge the thoughts and intentions of people's hearts. He showed me that when we attach motives to people's actions, in reality we are setting ourselves up as God. Those who attach motives to people's actions are doing so to find fault and it is done with the intention to stir others up to see that same fault. But it is God alone who is able to judge the thoughts and intentions of our hearts. The Lord knew my motives for painting my husband's former office. He knew whether I painted the office under false pretenses. He knew my guilt or innocence. And as I continued to listen, the Lord said, "Look at me! It is what I think that matters! I am the one who knows your thoughts and I alone can judge your motives. Do not look to what others have said. And do not allow this to bring fear to you as you carry on in this new church." I chose to stand in the truth. Truth is the key and foundation for not fearing man. When we are living in the truth it really does not matter what man thinks.

There are times a triggering event has snuck up on me, and other times I am well aware I am going into a situation which has the potential to trigger me. Although a triggering event is very painful and difficult to go through I have learned, surprisingly enough, not to fear it. I am able to embrace it because I know the Lord has more truth and healing for me. I always bring a triggering event to him. Without fail! I pray my way through them to healing. Although this is a place of heartache, tears and anger, it is also a good place. It is holy ground! God is at work! I know that when these triggering events happen, the Lord is saying to me: you are ready to receive more truth and healing. And my response must always be, "Yes Lord! I want to receive all that you have for me." I must allow him to speak his truth into the dark shadows of the trauma; to shed his light into my darkness and to breathe his life where there is death. Only then am I able to move out of the dark shadows of the trauma. It is here my soul is restored and God is glorified!

Chapter 6

SLOGGING TO FORGIVENESS

I realize there are entire books written on the topic of forgiveness. My one chapter is not going to shed new light on the issues. My main intent will therefore be to share what I've learned as I've worked to forgive those who pierced my soul. I thought of calling this chapter "A Journey to Forgiveness" but somehow calling it a journey made the process seem all too easy. For me, forgiveness was more of a slog! It was a schlep and a struggle. At the same time I do believe in miracles and I do not wish to take away from those who have experienced immediate and miraculous forgiveness toward others. But I believe more often than not, genuine forgiveness takes time and is laborious. One must work through an awful lot of muck, mire and pain. Slogging to forgiveness will look very ugly, and at times it may seem as though no progress is being made. But I believe no matter how messy it looks, it is pleasing to the Lord. He will be doing his finest work in the midst of the muck and mire.

Very early in the process leading to our departure from the church, I felt the tone of some meetings turning adversarial. I was quite perturbed with how I perceived we were being treated and so I went to my knees in prayer. As I prayed and laid out my grievances before the Lord, he broke into my thoughts and quietly said, *"Carol, as breath is to life so forgiveness is to spiritual life."* And then he repeated himself just to make sure that I had gotten it. I did not expect my complaining to be interrupted and I was caught off guard. I began to reflect on what the Lord said. These seemed like sobering words, but I did not spend too much time in reflection before I gallantly told the Lord that I choose to forgive. I choose life!

I am truly grateful that God reminded me of the importance of forgiveness months before we actually left the church as I had to consider these words many times. I am still not sure I really understand the fullness of what the Lord meant. Having grown up in the Church, the principle of forgiveness has been part of my life. I understand Jesus died to forgive the sins of mankind. Forgiveness is at the core our faith. Without forgiveness there is no salvation. I also understand that not only are my sins forgiven, but the sins of those who harmed me are as well. It is without question that I agree with and accept this. It is also part of my core beliefs that I am asked to forgive those who have trespassed against me.

Although these are the principles and beliefs I uphold, little did I know then how difficult it would be to remain in that place of forgiveness. Genuine forgiveness is not just saying the words *I forgive you* a hundred times a day with the hope that one day you might really mean it; that the words will finally give way to feelings of forgiveness. It is not some Christian mantra or slogan that must be incessantly repeated until the feelings of hatred or unforgiveness are gone. Forgiveness is a deep mystery that must be worked out in our heart, mind, spirit and deep within our wounded soul. I have had to confess my unforgiveness many, many times. And even as I write this book there are moments I stop in confession asking for cleansing and healing; then, I choose once again to forgive. I made a choice to forgive then and I am continuing to choose to forgive now. I live in the choice of forgiveness, though I confess, I am not yet living in its full victory. But I persist in the attitude and willingness to forgive, allowing the Lord to work in my heart until its completion. I continue to choose life!

I also recognize that when I make the choice not to forgive, I am in effect making myself God. And when I make myself God, with the power to forgive or not, I am rejecting God's salvation. In my self-deception, I reject God's standard for forgiveness and create my own. It is foolish to believe I hold the power of forgiveness. To deny someone forgiveness is to deny all that took place on the cross. The truth is I cannot hold someone to a different or higher standard than God's standard. This is what my head and my theology accepts, but at times my heart cries out *Crucify them! Crucify them!* My head understands forgiveness, but my heart wants punishment for those who trespassed against me.

I believe, in order to be able to forgive someone, we must come to a place of accepting what that individual has done. That is not to say we are to be accepting, or condoning the sin, but we must accept the *consequences* of the sin against us. The truth of the matter is we will have to live with the consequences of other people's sins against us regardless of our acceptance. The only choice we have is how well we will live. We may ultimately choose to live in unforgiveness and reap a life lived in bitterness and vengeance. This is a caustic and destructive choice and it will rob us of life. It is most certainly the choice that will eventually bring death to our spiritual lives.

As I considered forgiveness, I found myself struggling with what, for lack of a better word, I call the *integrity* of forgiveness. I have questioned whether we in the Church have really understood forgiveness. I wonder if we don't do a lot of pseudo or artificial forgiving. I do not believe we are fake or phony in our attempts to forgive one another. I believe most attempt to genuinely forgive from the heart. I wonder if, because we are Christians, we feel pressure to forgive one another and so we speak the words of forgiveness. But then we stuff down any angry feelings that arise when we think about our painful experience. I also think sometimes we forgive because of the expectations of others. But this kind of forgiveness is given to please a third party and in all probability it is guilt induced. We, the Church, cannot legislate forgiveness. It must come from the choice and heart of the wounded party. Pseudo or artificial forgiveness has no integrity; it falls short. Those who express forgiveness before working through their true feelings, will find their anger and guilt simply escalates. The issues never get resolved and though words of forgiveness may have been spoken, in reality there is no forgiveness.

I also wonder if we can fully forgive when we have not yet understood the consequences of a person's actions against us. If we extend forgiveness before we have experienced the consequences, we will find ourselves having to re-visit forgiveness again and again. I found myself in a position to convey forgiveness when I met with certain individuals just weeks after our departure. We had come together to clear the air and perhaps find a way to reconcile. I went to the meeting very confused and with little information as to what actually transpired. As we met together I gained a little more clarity regarding the actions these individuals had taken. But I did not gain a full picture nor realize the full implications of what they had done until much later. I know this does not sound Christian, but in retrospect, I wonder if I was a little too quick to offer forgiveness. Every time new information surfaced I found myself at the beginning again. I had to forgive them all over again because the new information dredged everything up again. It's left me wondering if I would have been better to wait until I had gained a clearer picture of the issues before offering forgiveness. Although I stand by the choice of forgiveness made then, I have also learned the lesson that perhaps it is okay to say that you need time to gain a sense of the whole picture; to think about and process the issues before you extend forgiveness.

Through my own difficulty to come to a place of forgiveness, I have gained great respect for those who have genuinely struggled to forgive someone even if forgiveness has not been achieved. I believe we, who come along side those who are working to forgive someone, must take care not to hurry the process along or to judge too hastily if forgiveness is not quickly offered. Although our intentions may be good and even admirable, we must be careful not to attach our expectations of what the forgiveness process should look like. We cannot insert our timeline for its completion. We may not recognize the depth of trauma suffered by those who have been wounded. We may in fact pressure them to forgive long before they are ready. In our haste, we trample on souls that are in agony and extraordinarily fragile. It is precisely because we as believers hold to the ideal that we must forgive one another, we may push others too quickly to forgive. And in the end, we may simply derail the forgiveness process through our expectations and impatience.

I have come to believe there can be so much damage done to one's soul that it is almost impossible to have the clarity or the ability to even begin to process forgiveness. Often emotions are just too raw and vulnerable. I have wondered if part of the key to forgiveness is to have our souls restored enough to work through to forgiveness. Some might contend that we need to forgive in order for our souls to be restored. This too is a valid argument. Perhaps it is both. Perhaps they must simply work hand in hand; as our soul heals we can more readily forgive, even as we forgive our soul is able to heal. I find myself still reflecting on this matter.

I've realized I have held genuine fears of forgiving those who wounded me. I feared that forgiving meant I would be forced to re-establish a relationship with the person who wounded me. But truthfully, I didn't ever want to see them again. I feared that forgiving meant they won again! Somehow I felt that those who injured me had victory over me. By not forgiving them I won! I had the upper hand. I gained back control. In essence, I felt that to withhold forgiveness was the only way I was able to punish them or hold them accountable for their actions because no one else did or could. I also feared that, if confronted, they would not acknowledge any wrong doing, or see the harm they caused and no apology would be extended. In doing so, I would just have more to forgive. And finally, I feared that if they were to apologize, that apology could not be trusted. It would just be meaningless and empty words.

I don't know how many hundreds of times I had made the choice to forgive those who wounded me. And once again,

I found myself in a place where I was struggling with anger and unforgiveness. And so I came before the Lord in prayer. I finally asked the Lord what it was that was holding me back from being free from my anger and unforgiveness. He said, *Cancel the debt.* As I reflected on this, I reasoned that when there is a debt, payment is owed. And I realized I felt those who harmed me, *owed* me something. Those who pierced my soul owed me and it was payback time! But the Lord was now telling me, it was time to cancel the debt. As I continued reflecting on this matter, I felt it important to make a list of what I felt was owed me. And so, somewhat in anger, I made my list.

- You owe me an apology.

- You owe my family an apology.

- You owe the church an apology.

- You owe me an explanation for your actions.

- You owe me genuine sorrow for the harm you caused.

- You owe me genuine repentance.

- You owe me to ask how you can make it right.

- You owe me to take responsibility for what you did.

- You owe me not to expect reconciliation just because you apologized.

- You owe me the respect not to touch me.

This list was made quickly and without too much thought. I wrote down the first things that popped into my head. The first nine items seem logical and justifiable but I was surprised by the last item on my list. What did being touched have to do with the debt owed? Initially I wanted to shrug it off. I felt I was just being silly. I took it off my list. However, I couldn't do it. I genuinely and strongly felt that I did not want to be touched by those who pierced my soul. I put it back on my list. But I couldn't understand why I had such an aversion to their touch. I wondered if it was an unconscious way to snub or hurt those who brought harm; perhaps a form of retaliation. It has since been suggested to me, when an individual has suffered abuse at the hand of another, they do not want to be touched. Am I claiming abuse? This word has been so loosely used in our culture that I think we no longer really understand its true meaning. If everything is abusive, nothing is. Please hear me; I am not claiming I was abused by those who were part of our removal. Yes, I was wounded deeply enough that I find myself physically wincing and even cringing at the thought of a touch or embrace by those who pierced my soul. But I've come to the conclusion that avoiding the touch of those who deeply wounded me is just an instinctive way to protect myself. I am not yet ready for their embrace.

With that in mind, I made a choice to once again forgive those who brought so much harm to me and my family. I then made the choice to cancel each debt owed; including the debt of not touching me. But several weeks after I made my initial list I was praying once again about an individual I continued to have difficulty with. As I prayed I felt the Lord calling me to cancel yet another debt.

- You owe me the debt of loyalty.

Whether we are conscious of it or not, we all have the expectation of loyalty in our friendships. Loyalty is the unspoken and unwritten rule in relationships. Like trust, it is part of the foundation of our friendships. Initially cancelling this debt seemed confusing to me. I had great and trusted friends in our former church. I thought I would be lifetime friends with some. But they took some actions which left me profoundly wounded. I felt betrayed. I also felt that my life and my family's life changed because of their actions. I certainly did not desire or require loyalty from the *friends* who betrayed me. Loyalty was no longer my expectation. Why cancel this debt? I was puzzled. As I continued to ponder the idea of cancelling this debt, I slowly began to understand. I believe the Lord asked this of me because my heart was broken over the loss of friends. And at the same time, I felt greater anger towards these friends than any others who had brought harm. I recognized that cancelling this debt was part of the acceptance of the consequences brought to bear through betrayal. Somehow this was at the crux of my soul being pierced. The Lord knew I could not move forward to freedom without cancelling this debt as well. But even today, I have to acknowledge, this continues to be a place of *stuckness* in my life. To this day I cannot understand why my friends chose to do what they did. And now the Lord was asking me to let go of the expectation of loyalty; the debt of loyalty in those friendships. I had to let go of the idea, that had my friends remained loyal, so much heartache could have be averted. And so in faith I simply chose to cancel the debt of loyalty that was once owed.

Although, I confess, while I would still like to see one or two items on my list of cancelled debts acknowledged and even acted upon, I have no expectation of that occurring. I admit, I have little faith in churches to take responsibility for wounds inflicted during divisions. I confess, perhaps at some level I chose to cancel the debt out of resignation that the Church does not pay its debts. But I will not and cannot wait for the church to act in order to find healing. My healing does not depend on the church paying their debts. I made the choice to cancel the debt for my sake, but above all, because it is pleasing to the Lord. It is what he asked me to do. It is part of the slog to forgiveness and part of healing. It is part of accepting the consequences and coming to a place of acceptance and peace. It is good and for my good. And it is for the glory of God. When I made the choice to cancel the debts I was given a gift to move forward in freedom. Today nothing is owed. The debt is paid. The balance is zero.

I have learned another great lesson from my struggle to forgive. When I read the story of the Good Samaritan I will no longer piously think that I would be the one who stops to lend aid to my injured enemy. I also know I would not be the one who crossed to the other side of the street in avoidance. No, I would be the one who saw the one injured, and I would go over and beat him more. I would be the one to pour salt in his wounds and say good riddance. Those who merely walked around the injured man are more righteous than I am. And when I read the passage of scripture about the servant who was forgiven a huge monetary debt; who then saw the one who owed him a pittance and demanded instant repayment, I would be the one who does the very same thing. But I would go even further. I would mock and humiliate him as I publicly berated him. You see when my soul was pierced it unleashed great hatred, anger and the desire for revenge. The Lord used the piercing of my soul to reveal to me what was hidden in my heart all along. I had just never been tested before. He needed to show me that there was self righteousness and murder in my heart. And so, I am no longer a judge over those who find it difficult or cannot forgive. I am no longer self-righteously looking down on those for whom forgiveness is as elusive as finding the pot of gold at the end of the rainbow. I have seen the hatred in my own heart and I have felt the rage of murder. I know what I am capable of. I know how difficult the slog to forgiveness is.

For a time after we left the church I was very confused. I was so deeply hurt and angry that I could not even consider partaking in communion. It was just a stinging reminder of the broken relationships I had left behind. I remember to this day when I felt I could once again partake in communion. That afternoon, the Lord spoke into my heart and I will never forget his invitation to come to his table of remembrance. How surprised and grateful I was that he wanted me to come. When I think about it, I am still moved to tears. And so, as I came to that familiar table, for the first time I really and truly saw my sin. I saw my guilt and the inability to change. I had not realized what I was capable of; what was buried deep within my heart. I was so broken and so in need of a Savior. I truly understood my need for mercy and grace. I had nothing to give; nothing to offer. I knew my sin. I saw my need. I came in brokenness. And I finally came in humility. There is no room for pride at the communion table.

My slog to forgiveness has been a long and hard struggle. And although it is not finished, I continue to make progress. As of yet there has been no miracle of love flooding my heart for those who pierced my soul. I hold no warm and fuzzy feelings for them. There is probably still a little desire for revenge left in me. But I have learned that I must live in what I call the *enoughness* of God's forgiveness. I have come to the conclusion that I have no desire or ability to forgive those who pierced my soul and any forgiveness I may offer comes from the Lord. He has enough forgiveness for the both of us. And as I look at Jesus in his enoughness, I am able to see him with his arms around me and at the same time, around those who pierced my soul. Yes, his arms are around those who wounded me so deeply. The Lord has never criticized nor spoken harshly about those who have brought so much harm. It is not in his character to gossip about them. He will not denigrate, or shame or humiliate them. They are after all, his children as well. And together, as we all stand before him, his gaze is fixed on me, and I hear him say, "I know! I know what they did. I know how much it hurt. I understand completely. But you have to trust me that I have *enough* forgiveness for the both of us." And I find myself weeping in the comfort and safety of his arms; and he, my Jesus, weeps with me. It is here that his love and my sorrow meet. And I am at peace. I see the compassion in his eyes and my heart and soul rest as he speaks his words of love, grace and mercy over me and yes, at the same time for those who brought so much harm. And so I choose to remain in that enoughness and I am strangely okay. I trust the Lord. He is enough! Yes, he is enough! And he has enough forgiveness for both of us.

Chapter 7

BEFORE RECONCILING

Reconciliation, by its definition, means to bring two or more people back into a relationship with each other after a dispute or estrangement. In its purest form, or perhaps better said, in its idealistic form, it is the restoration of a relationship after a conflict. Although a simple and unpretentious definition, in reality reconciliation is far from simple or uncomplicated. It is complex with many underlying issues. To even come to the place of agreeing to attempt to reconcile, is difficult and painful. Although I felt this book must contain a chapter on reconciliation, as I reflected on what I had written, I realized I was not championing the cause of reconciliation. As I took a closer look, I found I had written more about understanding reconciliation; specifically counting the cost and determining those it might be wise not to reconcile to. I believe one always takes a risk when reconciling and we are therefore wise to count the cost. There is a price to pay. Perhaps we may find the cost is too high.

As I have struggled to understand the issues involving reconciliation, I am left with more questions than answers. Questions like, how do you heal the wounds enough to even want to restore a relationship? How do you enter a process of reconciliation? Who should initiate contact? Is it the injured party's responsibility to initiate this process? Should it not be left to those who brought the injury to take the first steps in opening a door to reconciliation? But what if both parties are injured? Can the estranged parties handle the work of reconciliation on their own or would it be wise to have a mediator guide the process? Is reconciliation in fact merely a process to see whether trust can be rebuilt?

We as believers espouse a fundamental belief that reconciliation is an important part of church life and experience. Although we espouse the need to reconcile, in reality we rarely enter a process in which to resolve our differences. We think it is Christian to *forgive and forget*, to leave the past behind and move forward. We are masters at *sweeping it under the rug*. We ignore the issues and one another, choosing rather to live in the pretense that everything is okay. Instead of working towards a resolution in times of conflict and division, individuals or families simply move on to another church or stop going to church all together. As for the church, a new pastor is called and the hurts are never dealt with.

I believe that when a church has gone through conflict and division, ideally, some form or attempt at reconciliation should happen both at the corporate or church body level and at an individual level. I think of corporate reconciliation as being a body of believers agreeing to acknowledge their wrong doing towards one or more individuals. Although not everyone will have been a part of the conflict, they simply stand in agreement as part of the body of believers. This type of reconciliation would generally come in the form of a public apology. Idealistically, those at the forefront of initiating conflict and division would acknowledge their role in the dispute to the body of believers. I don't believe I have ever seen or heard of this happening.

It goes without saying that within corporate reconciliation is the need for individual or personal reconciliation. Division in the church always results in personal broken relationships. Corporate reconciliation acknowledges general transgressions whereas personal reconciliation deals more with the specifics of what occurred. It is where the nitty-gritty work of resolution and compensation actually happens. This process is private. It is far more sensitive and precise, and I believe very difficult to achieve. Rather than deal with reconciliation at a corporate level, my main purpose and focus for this chapter is to deal with the issues pertaining to personal reconciliation.

But before we can even begin to enter into understanding the principles of reconciliation, we need to understand forgiveness and reconciliation are two very different issues. We often want to marry them; thinking one cannot be afforded without the other. But they are not the same. They do not have to go hand in hand. Scripture charges us to forgive one another. We are asked to forgive even if it has never been asked for. But sometimes reconciliation is not possible. In Romans 12:18 we are called to, "if it is possible, as far as it depends on you, live at peace with everyone" (NIV). At times we may encounter those with whom we will have irreconcilable differences. Our reconciliation may look more like an uneasy truce, much like Esau and Jacob. They were re-united after years apart, but in the end, went their separate ways. Although we may question whether we can truly call their brief reunion, reconciliation, sometimes just being able to stand in the same room with someone or shaking their hand is in fact a form of reconciliation. I would add, even if a measure of reconciliation is achieved, it does not mean the relationship will look the same as it once did. It does not have to. Wounds may be too profound to enter into the depth of intimacy once shared. The truth is, we will not all reconcile according to dictionary or church standards and definitions. And I believe there are those to whom we should not reconcile.

I believe at the heart of reconciliation is trust. Forgiveness is given, but trust is earned. Forgiveness neither establishes trust nor does it equal trust. Trust is earned over a period of time; perhaps a long time. We will fully reconcile only if we can learn to trust again. Without trust you cannot have a relationship. You also do not and cannot love those you do not trust. Trust is the foundation of a friendship and the degree to which trust can be re-established may very well be the degree to which one can reconcile to another. When we forgive someone it does not have to include reconciling to them, but it goes without saying that we cannot reconcile without first forgiving one another.

As I have wrestled with the questions and the principles of reconciliation I've come to certain conclusions. These may be overly obvious, but nonetheless I believe they need to be stated.

In order to reconcile:

- Both parties must have a common understanding of what happened.

- Both parties must be willing to make the attempt.

- Both parties must feel safe.

- Both parties must come in humility.

- Both parties must be truthful.

- Both parties must take responsibility for their part in the conflict

- Both parties must take responsibility for the actions they took to cause harm.

- Both parties must forgive each other.

- The offending party *(parties)* must apologize.

- Trust must be re-established.

Early on, in an effort to both gain some clarification and find a measure of reconciliation, I briefly met with an individual. At our initial meeting they informed me that they had one hundred percent of the Lord's approval in what they did. They were in effect saying, "I am completely innocent of any wrongdoing and I neither acknowledge nor take any responsibility for the harm you experienced by my actions. Oh, and by the way, God completely agrees with me!" How do you argue with someone who has one hundred percent of God's approval? Although I did not say so at the time, I certainly did not agree with their declaration. Their perfection simply closed the door to further meaningful discussion or any hope of reconciliation for that matter. In my opinion this person had not come to our meeting in humility or truthfulness. We had no common understanding of what had taken place. If you cannot even come to an agreement as to what took place, there is no hope of reconciling. Unfortunately this attempt to reconcile fell short on just about every principle.

It is also through my own experience, I have come to believe, reconciliation is not a process that should be rushed into. Just as we may be tempted to hurry others along to forgive someone, we may push them to quickly reconcile. Again, we do so naively if we have not fully understood or taken into account the terrible harm one individual may have brought against another. We need to carefully weigh and consider the consequences someone has lived through at another's hand. It can take years before an individual may be ready to attempt to reconcile. Surprisingly, in retrospect, I would have been far more open to reconcile with those who wounded me within the first few months after leaving the church than I am today. Initially I was just both numb and stunned. I wanted to put the ugliness behind me. I wanted to get on with my life. Let's forgive and forget! Let's just kiss and make up! After all is this not the Christian way? However, I now realize this would have been premature as it would have left me with many unresolved issues. It took months before I felt like I had a clear grasp of what had really been going on behind my back. A few weeks after the fact was not enough time for me to realistically understand and begin to work through the consequences. Still in shock, I would have been far too quick to kiss and make up and then later realized there was so much more that needed to be said and worked through. I needed time to process what happened. I needed time to gain some perspective and physical distance. I needed time to gain emotional health. I needed time to access the damage, to be angry and time to grieve. I needed time to consider my own responsibility in what had taken place. I also needed time to reflect on those who I might choose to allow back in my life.

There are two Old Testament passages of scripture I have spent a great deal of time reflecting on. One is the story of David and Absalom found in 2 Samuel 13-18, and the other is the story of Joseph found in Genesis 37-50. I have found the lives of David and Joseph helpful in shaping my own thinking with regard to reconciliation. These were men who were greatly harmed by those they loved and trusted. And although they suffered terrible consequences, they remained faithful to God and to those who harmed them. Their lives amaze me and I find myself wanting to rise up to their level of integrity, humility and character.

The story of Absalom is found in the book of 2 Samuel. Absalom had a very beautiful sister named Tamar. Amnon, their half brother, fell madly in love with Tamar and longed to have her as his own. Amnon feigned an illness in order to have Tamar sent to his home to care for him. But as Tamar nursed Amnon, he raped her. Immediately after this rape, the undying love Amnon espoused for Tamar turned into intense hatred. He threw her out of his home. When Absalom heard about this he was enraged. He took Tamar into his own home where he cared for her. For two years Absalom remained silent about the rape, but all the while he plotted his revenge. When the opportunity finally arose, he murdered Amnon. Absalom then fled for his life. He left the country and became estranged from his father, King David. David grieved the loss of his sons; both the murdered one and the murderer. Three long years passed, and though he longed to be reunited with Absalom, King David steadfastly refused any such reunion.

David had a clever military leader named Joab. He realized how much David grieved over Absalom and so he hatched a cunning plan to reunite a father to his son. Joab's plan succeeded and David finally agreed to allow Absalom to move back to Jerusalem. But there was a catch; he was never to enter the King's presence. For two years Absalom abided by his father's decree, but finally he had had enough. He wanted to see his father. It was now time to end the estrangement. It was time to reconcile. How noble! How right! And so through some rather creative maneuvering Joab was summoned. It became his duty to convince King David to reconcile to his son. Joab successfully negotiated a truce and father and son finally came face to face. Ah! Reconciliation! How wonderful! Is this not the Christian ideal we all espouse? Absalom probably expressed deep sorrow and regret for what he had done. I am sure there were many tears shed and warm embraces as they reconciled. Perhaps Absalom gave an explanation why he murdered his brother; after all who wouldn't understand he had killed for the love and honor of his sister.

But the story is not yet over. There is yet another chapter in this tale of reconciliation. There was trouble brewing in the kingdom. You see, Absalom was not satisfied with just being reconciled to the King. No! Absalom wanted to be the king. He wanted the kingdom. It was the crown he had his eye on, and so he spent the next four years quietly undermining King David's reputation and authority through gossip, flattery and manipulation. He cleverly stole the hearts of the people away from God's anointed king; God's chosen one. And suddenly, Absalom declared himself King. Now it was David's turn to flee for his life. He was not about to fight his own son for the kingdom. He would not kill his son to keep the crown. David left quietly and humbly, never once uttering an unkind word against Absalom. I wonder what went through David's mind as he fled Jerusalem. David knew what he was facing. He had fled from Saul in his youth but alas, it was his very own son who chased him. And David was much older now. I have no doubt, memories of the hunger, the cold nights and damp caves, the loneliness and rejection, the fear and anxiety flooded David's soul as he, and those loyal to him, marched out of the city.

The kingdom had changed hands. It belonged to Absalom now. He was king! But he was not God's chosen! He was not God's anointed one! And though he gained the kingdom it was not through God's blessing. And even so, Absalom was not satisfied with just ruling this stolen kingdom. He could not let his rival, God's anointed, live and so he marched off after him. There was murder in his heart. God's anointed must be killed! But David! Ah, but David! He still loved his son, and on the day of battle he gave orders to deal gently with him. Deal gently with the one who stole the crown and the kingdom; who divided a nation. Soon enough the battle began. And as it raged, Absalom's hair got caught up in the branches of a tree. His mount carried on through the woods without him. And as he dangled helplessly in that tree, Joab came along. Joab had heard David's command to deal gently with Absalom. Had he forgotten the king's instructions? No, he had not forgotten, but even so, it was Joab who drew out his dagger and killed him. Joab, the same man who instigated and brokered reconciliation between a father and a son, now took the life of that son. And David grieved. He grieved deeply for the son who robbed him of the crown and kingdom.

David had paid a high price to reconcile to his son. I wonder, was the cost worth it? In the end it cost him the crown, the kingdom, it divided a nation and nearly cost David his life. Although Absalom insisted on reconciling with his father, he did so in pretense. He did not desire reconciliation because he loved his father. No, he loved the crown! At heart he remained a murderer; a manipulator, a thief, a gossip and a saboteur who subverted the rightful king's authority. And I wonder, did David ever question his decision to reconcile with Absalom? Had he not seen through Absalom's trickery as he manipulated people's hearts? Had he not recognized his character flaws? Had he not seen the signs? And do we realize, reconciliation not only held a personal cost to David, it cost the entire nation of Israel? A nation went to war! Was the price worth it? And interestingly enough, just as it only took one man to divide a nation, so too, it takes only *one* to divide a church. It takes one man or woman who thinks they should be king and a church will go to war.

And then there is Joseph! He was a cocky and arrogant teenager. He never held back telling his brothers about the rather lofty dreams he had and they despised him for it. They finally decided to kill him, but at the last minute they sold him into slavery instead. In Egypt, Joseph was bought by Potiphar, the captain of the palace guard. Scripture tells us that the Lord was with Joseph and he was successful in all he did. He was soon given responsibility to run Potiphar's entire household. Now Joseph, a very handsome young man, caught the eye of Potiphar's wife. She tried desperately to seduce him, but Joseph steadfastly refused to give in to her. Frustrated and angry with Joseph, she falsely accused him of attempted rape and he was immediately sent off to prison.

Not only had Joseph suffered the hardship and humiliation of slavery, he now suffered the injustice of imprisonment. But even in prison the favor of the Lord remained upon him and he was soon put in charge of prison affairs. In Psalms 105:19 we read, "Until the time came to fulfill his word, the Lord tested Joseph's character." He sat in prison for years! But Joseph chose to humble himself and trust in his God. When the time finally came to fulfill God's word, Joseph was called upon to interpret Pharaoh's dream. Pharaoh was so taken with him that he made him ruler over all of his possessions. Joseph went from prison to ruling a nation in one day. From rags to riches; from disgrace to honor in a heartbeat! He was given a wife and together they had two sons. The first born was Manasseh, meaning "God has made me forget all my troubles and the family of my father." The second son was Ephraim, meaning "God has made me fruitful in this land of my suffering." Although now years later, and a powerful ruler in Egypt, Joseph never forgot the day he was sold into slavery. That day was etched in his memory and deep within his soul. It was the day in history through which Joseph now viewed and lived his life. It was the BC and AD of his calendar. And every time Joseph called out to his sons was a reminder of a great injustice committed long ago. Manasseh and Ephraim would bear witness to their father's pain and sorrow for all generations to come.

But the story continues! There was drought in the land and as it persisted Joseph's brothers were forced to come to Egypt to buy grain. Joseph was in charge of grain distribution and as his brothers stood before him, begging for food, he instantly recognized them. But they did not recognize him. And so Joseph began to play a little game. Accusations of spying were made. There were veiled questions about the family. A strange demand was made to have the younger brother brought to Egypt. There was a brief, but private interlude of weeping. Finally a deal was struck! One brother would remain in prison while the rest returned to their home. They were given explicit instructions not to return to Egypt without the youngest brother, Benjamin. And so the grain was loaded on wagons; monies were paid but secretly returned. The long journey home was made.

It took some time and convincing before Jacob, their father, would allow the brothers to return to Egypt with Benjamin. But hunger finally forced the issue and so the long trip back to buy more grain was made. Once again the brothers stood before Joseph. All of them, including Benjamin. Overcome with emotion, Joseph again found a private place and wept. After gaining his composure, he returned to the banquet hall and lunch was served. More grain was purchased and again Joseph's manager was instructed to secretly return their money. Not only was the manager told to return the money, he was instructed to place Joseph's personal silver cup in Benjamin's sack of grain. When the wagons and donkeys were loaded, the brothers departed. But they had barely left the city when Joseph sent his manager after them, accusing them of theft and they were forced to return. "We're innocent," they cried! "We know nothing of the money or the silver cup!" But Joseph was adamant. The proof was in the sacks! And Benjamin, the one who had stolen the silver cup, would remain his slave. The rest could go home. After a sad and final plea from Judah, Joseph could stand it no longer. He broke down and wept openly in front of his brothers. His sobs were so loud they could be heard throughout the palace. Joseph had no choice but to reveal himself. His brothers were stunned and amazed at this revelation. There was more weeping and kisses all around! And all was forgiven! Joseph's father, brothers, their families and their herds were invited to come to Egypt with the promise Joseph would provide for them.

Is this not the happily ever after story we all love to hear? Well, perhaps… but I have questions to ask of Joseph! Why hadn't he checked up on or contacted his family after he gained his freedom and became a powerful ruler in Egypt? At the very least could he not have sent spies to gather some information? I want to know why he played mind games with his brothers. What were they all about? Was he toying with them? Was he trying to incite fear into them even as their actions had brought fear to Joseph? Was it initially his plan to have only Benjamin remain in Egypt? I wonder if he ever considered not revealing himself to his brothers. Was he tempted not to let them buy grain? Let them die! After all, death was what they wanted for him. And why was he overcome with such deep emotion; weeping with such intensity after so many years had passed? And did Joseph and his brothers really reconcile, or was theirs merely an uneasy truce? I wonder, because after Jacob, their father died, Joseph's brothers became afraid. They were worried Joseph would have them killed in retaliation for what they had done. They came to Joseph to ask for forgiveness for their actions. They claimed that on his deathbed, Jacob asked that Joseph pardon them. Was this the first time they apologized? Could it be that trust had never been re-established in their relationship? Joseph remained faithful to his word and assured his brothers there would be no judgment brought against them. Although Joseph was kind to his brothers and faithful to his word, was the memory of a murder plot just too much to overcome? Perhaps he had counted the cost and felt a truce was as far as he could go.

There is yet a third passage of scripture which I've found helpful in grappling with the principles of reconciliation. It's found in Ephesians 2:10-18. This passage tells us Gentiles were considered outsiders and were excluded from the Jews. Scripture says there was great hostility between them. But Jesus, through his death on the cross, reconciled both people groups to God and their hostility was put to death. He made peace by breaking down the "wall of hostility" which separated them. As I reflected on these verses I found myself continually coming back to the phrase, "the wall of hostility that stood between them." This passage is specifically in reference to the relationship between Jews and Gentiles but that wall seemed awfully familiar to me. I recognized it! I had raised it! I had to confess feeling deep hostility towards those who pierced my soul.

When we have been harmed we instinctively raise up walls of self-protection. These walls are both appropriate and needed. They give us safety. They give us time and distance to access our situation, to work through the pain and regain our footing. Even David, when he allowed Absalom to return to Jerusalem after years in exile, would not allow him in his presence for another two years. Although walls of self-protection are appropriate, there may come a point where they become walls of hostility. Walls of hostility will not allow reconciliation. They must be broken down to pave the way for reconciliation. But how are they broken down? How are healthy boundaries set up in their place? I meditated and prayed about this for a long time. Finally as I asked the Lord how to tear them down, he said, "They are broken down through humility." Yes, of course! I agree! It seemed simple enough. I needed to humble myself. It is then I realized that wounds are the building blocks that raise up the walls of self protection, but pride is the building blocks that raise walls of hostility.

Although I understood humility is the key for breaking down walls of hostility I struggled to understand what that practically looked like. My thoughts turned to a similar passage in Colossians 1:19-20 where it says, "For God was pleased to have all his fullness dwell in him, and through him to reconcile to himself all things, whether things on earth or things in heaven, by making peace through his blood, shed on the cross" (NIV). Here we read that Jesus reconciled us to God by making peace between us through his death. I finally came to a place of understanding that just as Jesus made peace between me and the Father, so too he is the way to peace between me and those who wounded me. It is not unlike the *enoughness* of forgiveness, where Jesus has enough forgiveness for all of us. When and if the time for reconciliation ever comes, the price has been paid. Jesus made the way and I will need to look at him, not at those who pierced me. I will have to trust that Jesus not only had enough forgiveness for the both of us, but he has broken down those walls of hostility and paved the way to peace. I will also have to trust that he will leave healthy boundaries in place.

We build walls of hostility to protect ourselves and keep people out, but in the end we just isolate ourselves. We cannot build new and healthy friendships when we are surrounded by hostile walls. But breaking down walls does not mean we must allow just anyone into our lives. It does not mean those who have pierced our souls must be invited back into our lives. I have come to the conclusion when a relationship is broken, we are given an opportunity, I would dare call it a gift, to consider if that person is someone we should reconcile with. We are given time to stop and ask ourselves if our relationship was healthy; was I healthy in that relationship. We are given time to evaluate the character qualities of those we are estranged from. We are given time to count the cost. It is my belief there are legitimate reasons not to reconcile with certain individuals; that is, to enter into a friendship again.

Throughout our lives we will have many kinds of friends. They will range from acquaintances all the way to intimate relationships. We will have many acquaintances; those we know at a distance. We will have fair-weather friends. Theirs is more of a friendship of convenience; usually the minute someone better comes along or there is conflict, they are gone. Other friends may be more like locusts. They come in, strip you and then they too are gone. They do nothing but take and give little if nothing in return. Theirs is a one-sided friendship where they reap all the benefits. They will strip you until there is nothing left to take and then they will move on to find others to consume. We may also find ourselves in a relationship with those who have certain character flaws, making them unsafe and even dangerous.

We are wise to learn how to recognize danger signs which should preclude certain individuals from our lives. It is wise to evaluate our relationships to see whether they are healthy. It is not wise to have friends who are there only to strip and consume us. We must guard ourselves against those who will just bring ongoing harm. It is one thing to be wounded by an individual who has made a mistake. It is quite another to be wounded by someone whose character allows them to not only repeatedly wound others, but justify and seemingly enjoy that behavior as well. We are also unwise to allow ourselves to have close relationships with those who are self absorbed and manipulative. They are frequently, performers. They are the drama queens who have some kind of crisis constantly swirling around them. You may recognize them when you find the conversation always revolves around them. They readily draw everyone into their stories and performance. They are interesting, intelligent and incredibly persuasive. They have the ability to almost effortlessly control others without them being aware they are being manipulated. They are charismatic, loads of fun and the life of the party. But they are in fact wily and most dangerous. They live by their own set of rules and there is no way to hold them accountable. When confronted, they may claim they are the victim, but it is more likely they are the victimizer. If your friendship has ended with such a person, you can be grateful. It was never a friendship to begin with. They have held all the power in the relationship, and although this may sound harsh, you were only there to follow and admire them. We would be wise to count the cost of all such relationships.

I believe it is wisdom to recognize that just because we have been reconciled to another it is not a guarantee for changed behavior. Although tears may be shed and promises made, only time will tell if change is genuine. It certainly is appropriate and right to clear the air or call a truce with those we are estranged from. But in the end, it may be wiser to go our separate ways. This may sound judgmental and unforgiving. It is not! What we are doing is setting up boundaries for our safety and well being. We are saying to them, "you cannot be part of my life because I am either not safe or not healthy when you are." These are limits or boundaries we can defend and we should feel no guilt in setting them. These boundaries are set, not in retaliation for the harm caused, but have to do with character qualities. Is it not wise to guard our lives from those who would just bring harm to us because it is in their character to do so? And is it not wise to weed out those who would just use us, consume us or manipulate and control us?

Although a few in our former church have expressed sorrow and regret and yes, even apologized for how we were treated, I do not consider myself to be reconciled to our former church; neither at a corporate level or at the individual level. No truce has been called. To date, there has been no acknowledgement, no apology and no responsibility taken by those who caused harm. I am unsure whether we even have a common understanding of what happened. I am learning to live with the unfinished and the undone and I am okay with that. I am okay with the fact that I still do not feel ready to face those who inflicted such deep wounds. I have realized my arms are not held out ready to embrace friends who harmed me. Instead they are still held out in a defensive posture saying, Stop! Don't come near me! Perhaps the wounds are still too deep. Although I am not yet ready to open my arms, I recognize the day may come when I will have to deal with those who pierced my soul. It will mean I must become vulnerable once again and truthfully, I still struggle with that. I believe those who wounded me deserve neither my vulnerability nor my trust. I paid a high price for their friendship, and right now, I have nothing left to give them. There is great truth to Proverbs 18:19 which says, "It is harder to make amends with an offended friend than to capture a fortified city." At this moment, I am not longing for those who I once considered friends. I am not asking the Lord to restore our relationship. I am however, praying that I would walk in readiness if and when the time should come where I am invited into a process of reconciliation. And I realize, if that time does come, I will have to make the choice to humble myself. My eyes will have to be on Jesus who humbled himself and paid the price for peace. But the reality is, although I will extend my hand to those who wounded me, for the most part, we will go our separate ways. For others, I will need to allow the process of reconciliation to reveal whether trust can be re-established. But oh, right now, even this seems so difficult, for just at this very moment, those walls of hostility feel so safe!

Chapter 8

ENEMY BLADES

Years ago the old adage *Sticks and stones may break my bones but names will never hurt me* was used as a comeback to someone's taunts against us. It was a popular saying and was considered to be a clever and witty comeback, but thankfully it is now recognized as being foolish and bearing little truth. Today we recognize words as having the ability to build someone up or tear them down. They hold the power both to bring good and to cause harm. Our words can be spoken in support and encouragement or to bring condemnation and shame. They can inspire someone to succeed or they can be so discouraging as to speak failure over them. Reckless words spoken over an individual will not be forgotten; rather they will imbed themselves in that individual's mind, eventually eating away at their soul. Words may not have the power to break bones, but they certainly have the power to rob someone of truth, hope, self-esteem and dignity, causing great harm.

Throughout this book and especially in this chapter, I have used the term *speaking over* someone. I have done so intentionally and perhaps it needs an explanation. I am using this phrase in the sense of words spoken that carry significant authority. We can simply have a conversation or *speak to* someone. But when we are in authority over, or are influential in an individual's life, our words carry greater weight. They hold power to affect that person's life to a greater degree. I believe we are empowered to speak *over* them. I believe it is also wise to consider the extent to which our words carry authority in the spiritual or angelic realm. A little understood example of this in scripture is where words spoken in blessing or cursing had authority to impact people's lives for good or for evil. Truly, this is a mystery. In our culture we know and understand very little of this. Perhaps it is something we need to take time to consider and reflect on further.

Some time ago a friend of mine was introduced to fasting; not from food but from words. I had never heard of a word fast and I was intrigued. I am a fairly quiet person and I really enjoy time alone. I do not feel the need to talk a lot. I reasoned a word fast should not be too difficult and yet I might reap some spiritual benefit. Yes, I admit, not the greatest motives! But I believe fasting to be a very worthwhile and beneficial spiritual discipline. And so with that in mind, I decided to fast from words for a day. I spoke only when absolutely necessary. I was only a few hours into the fast before I realized the immense life lesson I was about to learn. I was amazed how many words I actually used each day and how few of them were relevant and necessary. I became conscious of how often I had meaningless conversations. How often I gossiped, criticized or grumbled. I became aware of how self-absorbed I was, and how poor I was at really listening to others. In the days that followed, as I reflected on my past, I recognized how often I had used harsh or shaming words to discipline my children. I realized how often I spoke to others thinking I was being clever when in fact I was just foolish. I recognized times where adding to the conversation was unnecessary and even prideful. I was grieved as I came before the Lord and had to acknowledge the many, many words I've spoken foolishly and the harm I have brought to others through those words.

As I continued to reflect on the impact of our words, the Lord began to impress upon me that cutting, condemning or harming words are in fact *empowered* to wound. That is their goal and purpose. Those words become like swords or blades which pierce others, causing harm. The Lord also began to show me, that not only do destructive words come out of our mouths, but Satan will seize the opportunity to take those very same words and empower them to bring even greater harm. When Satan's accusations join with our harming words, together, they become a double edged sword of destruction. I believe James 3:6 speaks to that very issue when it says, "…the tongue is a flame of fire. It is full of wickedness that can ruin your whole life. It can turn the entire course of your life into a blazing flame of destruction, for it is set on fire by hell itself." This passage speaks to the fact that our words can be influenced and empowered by Satan. We should not be surprised by this for scripture warns us that Satan is "always prowling around like a roaring lion, looking for some victim to devour" (1 Peter 5:8). Revelation 12:10 says that Satan "accuses us before God night and day" and that "he is a liar and the father of lies" (John 8:44). He will constantly inundate us with his lies and half truths by throwing his fiery darts at us. Satan is not a paper lion. He is a liar and a thief. He comes only to rob, kill and destroy. We should also not be surprised that Satan especially attacks those who are wounded and weak.

As I reflected on this I was again sobered and deeply grieved when I considered not only the foolish words I've spoken, but how those same words then allowed Satan to inflict further harm on others. And once again I had to acknowledge, and in humility, repent before the Lord for the many, many times my reckless words were empowered to bring harm to others. In the past I have fasted from television, desserts and food in general, but I found myself most deeply impacted by the word fast. I consider the personal benefit and spiritual gain of this fast to be invaluable. That time of fasting heightened my awareness and sensitivity not only to the words I speak but how they may be heard. It has become much more important to me that my words be valuable, not just thoughtlessly gushing out. I am much more aware of what I say. I now take my words much more seriously. I am learning to guard my words and each morning I pray that, "…the words of my mouth and the thoughts of my heart be pleasing to you, O Lord, my rock and my redeemer" (Psalms 19:14).

As my husband and I faced the last few months of our tenure we both came under intense scrutiny and were strongly criticized. Although some might not agree, certain accusations made were neither accurate nor truthful. Some allegations may have carried grains of truth but they were nonetheless twisted and warped into something very ugly and unrecognizable. Was some of the criticism valid? Absolutely! Did we make some mistakes? Yes! But I knew I was not the person I had been accused of. Although serious accusations were leveled against me, I was never confronted, corrected or even rebuked by those making them. I am simply left to believe the accusations were made with the intent to injure and force my husband's resignation.

I recognized a lot of harming words were spoken over me

through the false accusations brought against me. Those harming words, lies and half truths had embedded themselves in my mind through the wounding I received. The Lord began to show me that I was not struggling with the accusations of men alone. Ephesians 6:12 says, "For we are not fighting against people made of flesh and blood, but against the evil rulers and authorities of the unseen world, against those mighty powers of darkness who rule this world, and against wicked spirits in the heavenly realms" (NIV). We must recognize that harming words not only come out of the mouths of people, but also from Satan. And because of the enemy's involvement, these harming words must be renounced both at the human level and at the spiritual level. For months I had made truth statements to myself to combat the condemning accusations made by men and women. I had renounced the lies and half truths which they had spoken over me. Although I had acknowledged the human element, I failed to fully recognize that Satan had empowered the accusations and lies to bring further harm.

When I finally saw the enemy's hand in the accusations brought against me, I understood why I had been so devastated. I now knew why I had been bowed low beneath the weight of criticism. I recognized the blade of certain individuals as it was empowered by Satan to bring greater harm. I recognized the double sided blade of destruction that had pierced my soul. And so in faith, I took my stand, and began to renounce the lies not only as coming from men and women, but from Satan as well. I renounced each lie spoken over me as they came to my mind. I renounced those coming from certain individuals and then I specifically renounced them as Satan's lies. I renounced them in the spiritual or heavenly realm.

Lord I renounce Satan's lie:

- I should feel shame.
- I deserve to be humiliated.
- I got what I deserved.
- My reputation is destroyed beyond repair.
- It was my fault my husband was asked to resign; was fired.
- Our time in ministry is over.
- I almost destroyed my family.
- I was spiritually manipulative and abusive.
- I was a secretive cult-like leader.
- I did not allow scripture to be part of the group I was involved in.

I renounced these lies and more. This list is not complete. Renouncing a lie that has some threads of truth woven in it will always be more difficult to combat than obvious or blatant lies. It is always harder to defeat a half-truth. Somehow they seem to carry more weight.

Because some of the accusations were so serious in nature, we submitted ourselves to our conference leaders for re-examination. My name was cleared, with some correction, and my husband's credentials were not removed. I believe most in our former church are unaware of the severity of accusations brought against me. I have not disclosed these accusations to open up a can of worms or to criticize those who made the allegations. I am much more concerned that as believers, we learn to recognize lies, false statements or half-truths spoken over us come from the pit of hell. Satan is the source, or at the very least, he has had a hand in it. We must renounce these lies as such, for this too, is a part of our healing.

1 Peter 2:15-16 says "It is God's will that your good lives should silence those who make foolish accusations against you. You are not slaves; you are free…" As I read this passage, I realized for a very long time I had been enslaved by the *foolish accusations* made against me. I continually felt as though I was living both in disgrace and under a cloud of suspicion. And although I knew the allegations made were not valid, somehow on the emotional level, I found it difficult not to believe that in some way they held some merit. I continued to be bowed low beneath the weight of criticism and accusation. The Lord reminded me of the verse of scripture, "Come to me all of you who are weary and carry heavy burdens, and I will give you rest. Take my yoke upon you. Let me teach you, because I am humble and gentle, and you will find rest for your souls. For my yoke fits perfectly, and the burden I give you is light" (Matt. 11:28-30). I was so very weary. And my soul desperately needed rest. I gave the Lord that ugly burden of criticism, of accusations and lies that for so long had weighed me down. It was not mine to bear. It did not belong to me; it never had!

There may still be those who feel I am who they have accused me to be. But it is God's judgment which will stand, not theirs. I have chosen to live a life that silences those who have made foolish accusations against me. Today I am learning to throw off the enslavement of those accusations and to live in the freedom that truth offers. I am continuing to refuse to allow the lies of others or the lies of the enemy to imbed themselves in my mind and soul. Lies and false accusations are not ours; they do not belong to us. We must own what belongs to us, not what others may think belongs to us. Lies and even half truths must never be believed. They cannot be allowed to penetrate our minds and embed themselves in our souls. Lies spoken over us will eventually shape us, leading us to believe things about ourselves which are not true. We must take the Lord's yoke on ourselves. We must allow him to teach us and set us free by his truth. Occasionally I find that I must once again renounce the lies spoken over me. There are days I somehow feel more vulnerable to hearing and believing them. But I continue to ask God to embed his truth in my mind and to cleanse me of lies that may have embedded themselves in my mind and soul through the wounding I received.

Although this chapter may seem somewhat strange, I have added it because I felt it very important to say, I believe healing from trauma needs to include spiritual warfare. Satan seizes the opportunity to take advantage of the weak and wounded and bring greater harm. Unfortunately, many of us in the Church have no idea how to stand against him. Some may have such a great fear of Satan that they would never consider taking a stand against him. Others may believe it is not possible for him to interfere with their lives. They therefore, never consider their suffering may in fact be part of Satan's schemes against them. Satan is not a paper lion; he is real and he is destructive. He is a thief and a murderer. He will try to affect our lives in any damaging way he can. But he has been defeated by the cross. We have authority in Christ Jesus to stand against him and his schemes. It is in Christ Jesus our Lord that we can overcome Satan's schemes and find healing.

Although we may be deeply wounded by harming words that have been spoken over us, it is imperative for us to remember that God does not speak destructive words over us. He does not speak accusing or condemning words over us. Even when he is correcting us, his words are full of love, truth and healing. They are life giving and full of hope. We, who have been wounded by the lies and accusations of others, need to remember, "The Lord your God is with you, he is mighty to save. He will take great delight in you, he will quiet you with his love, he will rejoice over you with singing" (Zephaniah 3:17, NIV). We need to believe our God rejoices over us. We need to know that he sings over us with joy. And when we allow him to speak his words of love and truth over us, we will find healing and rest for our souls, for he is mighty to save!

Chapter 9

BEATING SWORDS INTO PLOUGHSHARES

If I had the opportunity… NO!! If I had the courage! Yes, courage is the right word, for I am still filled with anxiety at the thought! If I had the courage to stand before our former church and describe my journey of hurt and healing to them, I would like to say something like this:

Dear church family,

The last time we saw each other was at the farewell lunch you held for us. Although this time was set aside to acknowledge and thank us for our many years of service, church was the last place I wanted to be. It was an awkward and difficult day. The pain of what we were put through during the final six months of our time with you overshadowed your kind words and well wishes. Although most of you bear little or no responsibility for that pain, our relationship has nonetheless been affected.

I want you to know, I have not written this book, or specifically, this letter, to point an accusing finger at you. I have not written to address what a good evaluation process or exit strategy should look like. I have no such advice to give. I have also not written with the expectation or hope we will come to a place of resolution and peace. I recognize our swords may never be beaten into ploughshares. Our relationship may never be fully restored. I have written this letter simply because it seemed fitting to do so. I felt there were some things I wanted to say; perhaps, needed to say. I realize it may have been wiser to speak to you in person, but the anxiety I still feel when I think about you will simply not permit it.

Many of you expressed concern with the evaluation process and with how badly things ended. I know the process of evaluating our tenure and future vision for the church weighed heavily on you. You did not take it lightly. I think we can all agree it would have been wonderful if this process honored God as well as one another. Unfortunately, due to the actions of some, it did neither. I still find myself perplexed as to why things deteriorated to the point they did. I believe we were all casualties of a flawed process and disappointing actions by some. Many of you expressed a sense of powerlessness not only to affect the tone of the meetings but the final outcome as well.

For those of you who thought it was time for us to go, I want you to know this was understandable and even appropriate. I

have absolutely no problem with this. But I do have a problem
with those who made our removal painful, demeaning and
humiliating. It was wrong! In their zeal to remove my husband
and implement a new vision, certain individuals inflicted deep
wounds which caused division in the church.

I don't know the full extent to which each person in the
church was affected, suffice to say, I know some left your
church to attend other churches. I wonder if you are aware
that some no longer attend church at all. Perhaps they are still
too wounded to entrust themselves to a church or perhaps
it has just become easier not to go. I also wonder if you are
aware that even I could hardly enter a church for at least two
years after we left you. It took another two years before I could
sit through a church service without feeling overwhelmed
by anxiety. I just wanted to run out and never look back.
It saddens me that your church remains on my list of last
places on earth I want to be. I have great apprehension and
anxiety when I consider the fact I may one day have to return.
And yet strangely enough, though I consider our relationship
strained and even broken, rarely a day goes by that I do not
think about you. Years have passed and you remain in my
heart. I am immensely grieved over the fact my family cannot
slip into the back seats to worship with you without causing
severe stress either to me or to some in your congregation.

I am sure you can understand that it was very difficult for
me to hear my family's faults and our future being discussed
and even argued about. I found it humiliating to be publicly
criticized and denigrated. We were discredited and our
reputations were tarnished. As the harshest criticism was
leveled at us, I chided Brad for not defending us. He turned
to me and said, "God called me to shepherd this church and I
will not now turn and attack the very sheep I was entrusted to

teach and protect!" I will never forget those words. Although he could have defended himself it would have come at the cost of others. He was not about to bring public criticism against those he had served with and shepherded for so many years. I want you to know he lived that even at home. He remained and continues to remain faithful to you. Martin Luther King once said, "The ultimate measure of a man is not where he stands in moments of comfort and convenience, but where he stands at times of challenge and controversy." Although my husband was severely criticized, his reputation tarnished and his career was put in jeopardy he stood before you as a gracious man, full of integrity; guarding the sheep entrusted to him. I was never more proud of him than at this moment. Today he remains a man of integrity who faithfully serves the Church.

Perhaps in the future, if you find yourselves once again evaluating your pastor's tenure, you might consider taking a few words of wisdom to heart. Know that this will be a time of challenge and controversy. It is therefore wisdom to guard your hearts and your words. Valid criticism is good. It is needed and useful, but there is a time and a place for it. When the church's vision or your pastor's tenure is being evaluated, it is showing wisdom to not be too quick to add your voice to the chorus of criticism and accusation. It is all too easy to get caught up in the frenzy and join others in casting aspersions. But words spoken in haste and in the heat of the moment cannot be taken back. It is also wise to consider the fact that hasty judgment sets the trap for injustice. I believe it is also wisdom to take time to consider if you are being used to achieve someone's agenda. Perhaps empires are being built among you. And lastly I would add, though you hold the power to condemn perhaps it is wise, or at the very least, it is showing mercy, to put down your stones and to sheath your swords.

Although I was profoundly wounded through the process of our departure, I want you to know that I have no expectations of you to respond to or take action for the pain I found myself in. I do not expect you to bind up my wounds and I do not expect you to be part of my healing process. My healing does not depend on you at all. I am not asking for an apology or compensation of any kind. And yet having said that, have you ever considered that an apology might be the right thing to do? Our swords cannot be beaten into ploughshares without one. Restoring our relationship hinges on an apology. And I suppose if I am truthful, I believe an apology would be appropriate and even nice. On the other hand, I find myself anxious at the thought. Why? Because even after all these years I do not feel ready!

Perhaps in the future, a time may come that you as a church and I may feel it appropriate and necessary to come together. There may come a day when we will beat our swords into ploughshares. I suppose the starting point will have to be an apology; perhaps on both our parts. I very much appreciate what Randy Pausch has to say about both good and bad apologies in his book *The Last Lecture*. I believe his thoughts on this matter are wise and warrant consideration. He says a bad apology includes these kinds of statements:

- "I'm sorry you feel hurt by what I've done." [1]

- "I apologize for what I did but you need to apologize to me for what you've done." [1]

According to Randy, by saying, "I'm sorry you feel hurt by what I've done," an individual recognizes the wound but offers no salve for healing. They do not take responsibility for their harmful actions and offer no comfort. Secondly, Randy says an apology that is given but has a demand for an apology tacked on, is not an apology. In reality it is asking for an apology. A genuine apology needs to be based on the actions taken which offended or wounded an individual. It cannot be based on what was done to you. They are separate issues. In the end, the individual who makes a bad apology takes little or no responsibility for the harm caused. They will do only the bare minimum in hopes of a quick resolution.

Randy Pausch goes on to say that a proper apology includes three things:

- "What I did was wrong."[1]

- "I feel badly that I hurt you." [1]

- "How do I make this better?" [1]

Within these words lies contrition. Salve is offered for the wound. Responsibility is taken. This apology acknowledges the actions that brought harm regardless of what the other person did. It keeps what they did and what the other individual did, separate. It says "I am sorry that I injured you and I am willing to live with the consequences that will make this right." If you add conditions or excuses to your apology, you will have greater resistance to forgiveness and reconciliation. When someone apologizes in humility and contrition, it makes forgiving easier. It also cracks open a door of trust.

In closing I wanted to share with you some thoughts from my son Derian. He was deeply traumatized as he faced first our resignation, and then his own as your youth pastor. For a time we did not know if Derian would ever be in ministry again. Today he is a remarkable young man with a heart for God and an amazing ministry.

This is a posting from Derian's blog:

> The June 2010 cover of TIME magazine headline reads "Why Being Pope Means Never Having To Say You're Sorry". I happened upon it while rushing to an ATM in a convenience store. The restaurant I had just eaten at took cash only and I only had plastic. To make matters worse I had brought a number of youth along with the promise that I would pay for the meal. So while my young friends awkwardly hung-out at our table, I rushed to my car and drove like a madman trying to find an ATM. It is funny how easily distracted I can be. This magazine caught my eye and I forgot about what I was supposed to be doing. I pulled out my phone and snapped a picture. Eventually I did remember and got the cash, returned to the restaurant and paid the bill.

> So what was it about this cover that stopped me in my tracks? It wasn't the Catholic Church's sexual abuse scandal that I resonated with. It wasn't the Pope's unwillingness to apologize. I saw a much deeper, more universal issue. It was the church's (Catholic, Protestant, Evangelical, Liberal, Anabaptist, Independent, Para church…) unwillingness to confess their sins and ask for forgiveness.

> I will admit that perhaps my view of church has been skewed or rather scarred by a few people who hurt me deeply. It is something I have wrestled with for many years now. There was a time, because of my wounds, when I wanted nothing to do with God and

especially not his Church. Over the years God has healed my wounds and brought me to a great church, not a perfect one, but a good one. I still walk with a limp, but I see much clearer. I believe God has used my wounds to teach me much about myself and his church. I might even go so far to say that I am glad for the wounds but it has been a long and dark road to be able to speak those words as of yet.

I empathize deeply with those who are frustrated with the Church; who've been hurt by the Church and who've become disappointed with God because of the church. One thing I've learned is that hate toward one church quickly spreads like a cancer toward the whole church and eventually toward God. Most atheist's I've talked to have stopped believing in God rather than never believed in God-often because of very negative experiences with religious people. I believe this is one reason why humility and confession are such an important practice for the Church. At times we've done good things (like Evangelism) in bad ways and hurt people. At times we've done bad things (like Legalism) with good intentions and hurt people. James 5:16 says, "Therefore confess your sins to each other and pray for each other so that you may be healed." We need to wake up to the fact that there are a lot of walking wounded both inside and outside the Church. Maybe you weren't the one who hurt them but perhaps you can be the Good Samaritan in their life.

Donald Miller in his book, *Blue Like Jazz*, tells a story of how confession began to change the university he attended. Every year his school celebrated a week of debauchery—anything went. He and his friends decided to set up a confessional booth in the middle of campus with a sign outside that said "confess your sins." They dressed as priests, pastors and monks and waited for people to come. Inside the confessional booth, the priest would then confess the church's sin—the inquisition, the holocaust, racism, witch hunts, homosexual hatred etc. With tears in their eyes people would leave the booth and run to get their friends. It was a transforming moment.

I have experienced the power of confession first hand. It was the day I went back to my doctor to refill my anti-depressant prescription. I had sunk into depression shortly after resigning as youth pastor. After a year symptom free I stopped treatment but soon the darkness returned. On my way home from the doctor's office I had to drive past my old church. I decided to see how the church secretary was doing. As we were chatting, the new pastor popped in and asked if he could talk with me. He talked for a long time about what he was doing with the church. I was wondering why he was telling me this, when he stopped and said, "So the question I have for you is… What if anything does this church need to do to be in right relationship with you?" I broke down in tears in this stranger's office. He was the first person to acknowledge my hurt and he had nothing to do with my wounds. I don't know what happened that day but I walked out of that room a changed man. That night I went to take my pills but something inside of me was different. That was years ago and I still haven't touched those pills. I was healed by a stranger who humbled himself on behalf of others and sought to make amends.

I guess what I've been trying to say is perhaps what the world needs from us Christians is less Apologetics and more Apologies.

Derian and I... our family shares this blog with you because we want you to know we are okay! Our family is doing well, though as Derian said, some of us still walk with a limp. We have come through a very difficult and dark time, but we are moving forward. We are healing and our souls are being restored.

I also want you to know you are forever in my heart!

Carol

PS: My sword is sheathed though it is not yet beaten into a ploughshare. Perhaps one day it yet will.

ENDNOTES:

1. Randy Pausch, Jeffrey Zaslow. *The Last Lecture*. (New York: Hyperion,2008), page162.

Chapter 10

MY SOUL MUST SING

Years have passed since our departure from the church; since my soul was pierced. And although I would like to think so, I am quite certain my journey of healing is not yet over. There is still pain. There is still some anger. I have not gone back to our former church. Our relationship remains undetermined at best. I've not spoken with those who sought our removal. I've have had no contact with the individual I turned my back on and walked away from. I've not faced those who brought accusations against me. These relationships remain broken. And I am learning to live with the unfinished and unresolved. I am fully aware there may never be a resolution and for now, I am at peace.

When my soul was pierced, words fell utterly short. They failed to express the depths of pain, sorrow and anguish I felt. For a long time my soul was unable to sing the joyful song it once sang. I groaned in agony and wept in confusion and pain, in grief and anger. My soul thrashed and moaned as if in the throes of death yet fighting for life. But this song of despair and sorrow; this mournful dirge is finally subsiding. My anger and sorrow is diminishing. The constant flow of tears is lessening. My weeping is turning to joy. My soul is healing. It is being restored by a gentle healer; my Savior and friend. I am not the same person I once was. I have been humbled and broken. I have been re-shaped. I am finding my footing once again, though I still walk with a bit of a limp.

I have finally found the words with which to express the hurt, pain and grief and yes, the damage done. But it has not been an easy road. I have learned healing does not automatically happen, rather, it is grueling work. This journey has not been one taken in haste. And often it has been a lonely, grief filled place. It is as though grief begets loneliness. It is difficult to invite or even trust others with your grief. They cannot work out your grief for you. You must work through the pain and loss.

At the same time this has been a holy place, for God has been at work. He has been cleansing and healing my broken heart; restoring my soul. The Lord has given me wisdom and insight into the damage done to my heart, mind and soul and has brought me to places of acceptance and peace. But I have had to allow the Lord to take me where at times I did not wish to go. I have had to put my hand in his as he has helped me come to terms with the final six months of our tenure. I have had to choose to sit at his feet and allow him to open my eyes and ears to his truth. I have had to give him my heart that has been unforgiving, embittered and hard. I have had to give him my soul that at times writhed in anger, anguish and grief; begging that no one be allowed to touch it for fear that even the most delicate caress may cause it to shatter beyond repair. And God has been faithful; treating me with great tenderness, with compassion and dignity. Never has he run ahead of me bidding me to hurry. Instead he has walked stride for stride as I have been ready to face each step necessary for my recovery. Progress has often been slow and painful. Surprisingly, this process has been so painfully slow that I am often the one who has run ahead of him thinking I was ready to take a new step. But his timing is always perfect and I have had to rest in his wisdom to take as much time as I have needed before each new step was taken. There are no short cuts here and there is no room for pride. Pride simply closes the door to healing.

I have learned God delights to take the wounded and the broken and bring his healing. He longs to be gracious; to redeem our past and restore our souls. I found he never once made light of my wounds; he always acknowledged the depth of pain I was in. I also found that God is persistent and thorough. And though a gentle healer, he allows us to live in great pain for a very long time. I've learned healing is and will always be my choice. God will only take us down this road as we give him permission to do so. I have had the choice to refuse his healing. I have also learned, regardless of how much or how little others are to blame for the consequences I am living in, I am responsible to work through those consequences and pursue the healing and freedom God has for me. I am responsible for the actions I choose to take in response to the piercing received.

I believe many who have been pierced in their soul make a courageous and genuine effort to find healing. But a full recovery is often obstructed by overwhelming confusion, grief, anger and trauma. All too often this journey ends prematurely and there is never a full recovery. I believe many live in avoidance; ignoring the pain. They refuse to be introspective because they simply cannot bear to look at or feel the pain again. But as debilitating as it may be, and as much as we may try to skirt around or deflect the pain, for healing to take place we must allow the Lord to take us through the pain and through the damage. If we choose not to walk through the devastation and hurt; if we choose to ignore it, we are left susceptible to spiraling into a place of anger, self-pity, unforgiveness, bitterness, and plotting revenge.

We who have been deeply wounded must understand our experience and the ramifications of it in order to process and move beyond the pain and loss. I have learned there is great benefit in seeking professional counseling. When seeing my counselor, I prayed for the Lord to guide the conversation. I prayed before my appointments and after them. I read the books and did the homework assigned to me through my counselor. Without counseling I would not have understood how deeply traumatized I was. I would never have known I was suffering from PTSD. Without this knowledge I would still be triggering without understanding the reasons why. I would still be living under the dark shadow of death that trauma had cast over me with the repercussions of unresolved hurt continually reverberating in my life. I would have remained in the place where my soul was robbed of the joy it once knew and the song it once sang. We, who are in need of healing, must find refuge under the shadow of God's wing. It is here that his love and our sorrow meet. And it is here our souls will learn to sing their joyful song once again and our feet will learn to dance again… even if it is with a slight limp.

Although I benefited greatly from counseling, my healing has largely been brought about through prayer. I prayed and prayed and prayed. I brought everything to the Lord. I hid nothing from him. The Lord desires truth in our inner being. He can handle the truth no matter how dark and ugly. And after I prayed, I listened. I listened for what the Lord wanted to say. I did not do all the talking. I gave the Lord opportunity to speak into my life. I intentionally asked for his wisdom and any instruction he may have had for me. I always asked that I would be teachable; that I would have ears to hear and that I would be obedient to whatever the Lord asked of me. Sometimes I spent months praying about a certain issue I struggled with. Receiving insight or even a measure of healing rarely came instantly. I fasted where I could, although I found fasting under these circumstances very difficult. But I was constantly amazed how much the Lord did with how little I was able to give or do.

In the movie *The Count of Monte Cristo,* great betrayal and injustice had been committed against Edmond Dantes. He received an undeserved life sentence to be served in a terrible prison. No one left that prison alive! As Edmond entered his cell he saw the words *GOD WILL GIVE ME JUSTICE* etched into the stone wall by a former prisoner. With confident faith Edmond continued to carve the words even deeper into the stone. But after years of isolation and suffering, Edmond's longing for justice turned to despair and a desperate need for revenge. Years into his prison sentence, a fellow prisoner, tunneling his way to freedom, surprised Edmond when he accidently popped up in his cell. The two became friends and together they continued to tunnel their way to freedom. Priest, as he was called, was a God fearing man, who educated Edmond and tried to dissuade him of his zeal for revenge. Tragically, nearing freedom, their tunnel collapsed and Priest was mortally wounded. Priest encouraged Edmond to carry on tunneling to freedom and when he gained it not to waste his freedom on revenge. His dying words to Edmond were,

"Do not commit the crime for which you are now sentenced. God says, 'Vengeance is mine!'" These are wise words. When we carry out our revenge or repay those who have wronged us, we become exactly what they have accused us of, and what we have been imprisoned for. And I believe far worse, we become just like them.

I have often watched this movie. To this day it touches the deep and sorrowing parts of me. I am always moved to tears and I am always moved to reflect upon my own progress toward healing. I've learned what a miracle it is to forgive someone who has wronged you and greater miracle yet, to be reconciled to them. In my humanness I desire harm toward those who harmed me. But 1 Peter 3:9-12 implores us not to repay evil for evil and warns us not to retaliate but instead to bless. And so I've learned to have the attitude of scripture where it calls us to bless if we are harmed. I've learned to sheath the sword of revenge and leave vengeance in the Lord's hands. Some days that choice is very half hearted and I simply acknowledge that before the Lord. I choose to trust the Lord to take the actions he sees fit and recognize that I need to deal with what the Lord is pointing out in my own life. I've learned that I must keep my eyes on the Lord.

The unhealed wounds in our past can choke out all joy in life. They can choke out God's abundance. We cannot change the past. We cannot undo what has been said or done. Although I would never willingly choose to be pierced in my soul, or incur the many consequences brought on by this wounding, today I can genuinely say that I am grateful for what I've gone through. Today I can say the soul piercing I received was in truth a gift from God. Yes, it came disguised in a most cruel and ugly form. And yes, it caused undeniable and permanent damage, but in the Saviors hand, what men, women and demons used to bring harm, God used to bring healing, transformation, life and his goodness. No matter what evil we have done or what evil has been done to us, God desires to bring good out of it. This is not an empty promise but something to put our hope in.

Throughout this time of wounding and pain, I have been constantly reminded that God is good. We, who are in pain, must believe and trust in the goodness of God. The truth is, in all things God is good! If wounding and loss has come, it has come with God's permission and with great purpose. And God is always good! Both David and Joseph endured years of suffering, refining and testing. Years passed as the Lord not only searched, but tested their hearts. Years passed and the promise of kingship and lofty dreams of honor were long forgotten. But God had not forgotten! His word, his truth stands the test of time. On the day Joseph was sold into slavery, he was not told that God would one day use him to save a nation. On the day David fled from Saul, he was not told that his songs and poetry would be part of scripture for all time. He was not told that the Messiah would come from his line. The years of slavery and prison; the years of fleeing and cave dwelling had taught Joseph and David that God was greater than their circumstances. They learned to know the God who would use the evil actions of others to preserve a nation, and set in place a kingdom without end. They learned to know the heart of God. They learned humility, obedience and faithfulness. They learned to be men of honor in places of great dishonor. And like Joseph and David, we who find ourselves in places of dishonor need to know God is with us. He is for us! He has not forgotten us. He has not abandoned us. We are being tested in the refiner's fire and we must have faith that one day we will rise up out of the ashes in victory. We who have been threatened or mistreated; we who have suffered loss must learn humility, faithfulness and obedience. We who are dwelling in damp caves and fleeing for our lives must live in the hope of a God who is faithful. God is greater than our circumstances and he is greater than those who brought harm. Will we submit even if it takes years? Will we humble ourselves and learn? We may grow impatient, thinking these years are a waste. But God does not waste our time! Years of refinement and discipline are never wasted. In fact, I believe these years are more important than any years of fruitful ministry. They are there to develop in us an authentic trust in the Lord, an intimacy with him, and a deep and abiding love for him. They are there to make us more like our King. We do not know today, how God might want to use our lives for tomorrow. We do not know what *nation* will be preserved because we have submitted our lives to him and have lived in faithful obedience. We do not know where God's kingdom will be established because we have humbled ourselves, believed God and obeyed him.

I awakened one morning feeling rather teary and upset. As I came to the Lord in prayer, he began his work of healing once more. The darkness and oppression was lifted off of me as he brought his truth and healing to my soul once again. Later that afternoon while working on this book, words began to pour out of me. They came from the deep and healing places; the places of life within my soul. Words which for so long had eluded me, tumbled out almost effortlessly onto the page. And a *psalm* was born; my psalm! I love the Psalms. I love David's honesty. I love his loud protests. I love his insistence that the Lord come to his aid. I love that no matter how dark and deadly the day, David's voice rises in praise to God. David understood, without question, in all things, and in all ways God is good and worthy of praise. But I also love David's rants against his enemies; his cries for God to destroy them. And just who are these enemies? Are they merely human enemies or can they also include the demonic forces? We aren't told. But I believe this fury spouted against the enemy may actually include both. I personally, find the Psalms helpful in leading me to stand against Satan and his schemes.

The psalm that poured forth that afternoon became my shout of victory. It is my joyous victory dance! It is a shout of praise to my king, my healer, my deliverer and my faithful friend. But it is also a rant against my enemies, whether they are human or demonic is left for you to decide. Listen! And you will hear my soul sing once again as I stand under the shadow of his wing. No, it is not the same song I once sang. It is a new song! Its melody has been burnished by refining fires. This is a song of praise to my friend, my Savior and King; to God, who is mighty to save! May his name be lifted up and may he be glorified!

My Soul Must Sing!

A Psalm of Praise

Oh Lord, you are my God!
You are my stronghold; my deliverer.
My soul cried out to you and you heard me.
You came and rescued me.
When the sword of accusation pierced my soul
it passed through you first.
You shielded me from its fatal blow.
You allowed men's foolish accusations to test my heart.

And their reckless actions revealed what was in theirs.
You did not abandon me to their slander.
You did not allow me to be enslaved by their lies.
You untangled me from their web of half truths.
You placed me in your refining fires
to reveal any hidden sin in me.
Your flames brought truth and cleansing.

When my reputation was tarnished
you lifted my head high.
When my name was dishonored you said,
"Stand tall my child."
When I was struck down in betrayal
you remained at my side; forever faithful.
You carried me when I could go no further.
You are my shield and defender!
My strength! Heart of my heart!

You guarded my life from the enemy's wrath.
Those liars!
Brandishing their terrible blades of destruction!
How I hate them!
You opened my eyes to see their trap set for me.
You exposed their web of deception.
They thought they could veil me in confusion
and shroud me in guilt.

They wanted my destruction. They showed no mercy!
They sought to rob my soul of its joy.
They tried to silence the song I once sang.
My soul does not belong to you,
you liars, you robbers!
Do you think you can take what does not belong to
you and God will not notice?
Do you think that he does not know what you are
plotting?
Do you think he is fooled by your lies?

Should I fear you?
You are cowards!
Hatching your cruel plans for destruction!
Your treacherous schemes are devised in secret
and shrouded in darkness.
But I will not fear you! I will not fear man!
I will fear God alone, for it is his word
and judgment which will stand.
And as for you, the feather in your cap has become
a millstone around your neck.
Your blades of destruction have been turned back on
you.
Your swords of injustice, silenced!
My enemy did not triumph over me,
for you oh Lord, heard my cry and rescued me.
Great is the Lord! He is my deliverer!

He is my shield and defender!
My strength! Heart of my heart!

I have passed through the flames of refinement.
In safety I have walked past the traps set for me.
The veils of confusion have been rebuffed by truth.
The shrouds of guilt have given way to joy.
How great are you oh Lord!
How great is the heart that rescued me.
Yes! Great is the Lord! I will offer up my praise to
you, my Savior, my friend.

When my heart was consumed by fear
you spoke of your love for me.
You delighted in me.

When my thoughts were stuck in the quagmire of
endless repetition, you gave me living water to drink.
You fed me with your truth. You said, "Be at peace."

When I was bowed low beneath the weight of
criticism, you spoke words of affirmation.
You placed me on the solid foundation of your truth.

When I felt naked with shame,
you clothed me with robes of dignity.

When trauma cast its shadow of death over me,
you shone your light in my darkness.
You spoke words of freedom and hope over me.
You declared your victory for me.
In your mercy, you brought healing to my brokenness.
You restored my soul and your name was lifted high.
And so my soul sings your praise!
My feet dance in joy for you are my king!
You are my shield and defender!
My strength! Heart of my heart!

Oh Lord, guard my heart from plotting evil against
those have sought my ruin.
Do not let me reconcile with those who desire to
bring their destruction yet again.
Do not let me be tethered to evildoers.
I want nothing to do with them.
Guard me from opening the guestroom door to
bitterness.
This door of compromise must never be unlocked.
Do not allow unforgiveness to take root in my heart
and choke out your abundance.
Do not allow the unquenchable flames of anger to
rule my life.
Guard my heart from holding grudges against those
who pierced my soul.

Let your forgiveness reign.
Let me rest in your justice.
Let me live in your peace.
Let my soul ever praise you!
Yes, I will praise you, for you are my deliverer!
You are my shield and defender!
My strength! Heart of my heart!

My head does not droop in shame.
It has been lifted high in praise.
My shoulders are not slumped in disgrace.
I stand tall in your mercy.
No longer will my soul sing its mournful dirge.
For your love oh Lord, and my sorrow have met!
Oh my soul! You have thrown off the robes of grief.
Your sorrow has turned to joy.
The time of weeping has ended!
My soul will arise in praise to you oh Lord,
singing its joyful song.
You are my shield and defender!
My strength! Heart of my heart!
Oh my soul, sing in victory!
Lift up your voice!
Shout!
Let everyone know!
It is well with my soul!

Made in the USA
Charleston, SC
26 February 2012